A Life Remembered:

A Memoir of Anew McMaster

To John, Jenny, Brigid, and David

A Life Remembered:

A Memoir of Anew McMaster

Mary-Rose McMaster

Carysfort Press

A Carysfort Press Book in association with Peter Lang
A Life Remembered: A Memoir of Anew McMaster
By Mary-Rose McMaster

First published in Ireland in 2017 as a paperback original by
Carysfort Press, 58 Woodfield, Scholarstown Road
Dublin 16, Ireland

ISBN 978-1-78874-684-7
©2018 Copyright remains with the author

Typeset by Carysfort Press
Cover design by eprint limited

Caution: All rights reserved. No part of this book may be printed or reproduced or utilized in any form or by any electronic, mechanical, or other means, now known or hereafter invented including photocopying and recording, or in any information storage or retrieval system without permission in writing from the publishers.

Contents

Acknowledgements	*viii*
List of Photos	*Ix*

Introduction		1
1	Birkenhead, the Early Years	11
2	London, a Mentor and a Significant Meeting	16
3	The Willmores	21
4	Mac, Mana, Micheál, and the First World War	26
5	Vanished to Australia	32
6	An Arabian Prince Returns, and '*Iris*'	37
7	Flight into Ireland	41
8	First Tours, and Micheál and Hilton	45
9	Shakespeare at the Abbey	53
10	A Second Abbey Season	60
11	Williamstown, and Mrs Patrick Campbell	65
12	Hard Times	70
13	Stratford	75
14	Chiswick	83
15	Religion, Scotland, and the Second World War	89
16	Loughleven Cottage	95
17	Touring During the War	98
18	Lord Longford and Oedipus	104
19	Fire, Lights and the War	109
20	Facts of Life	114
21	Burgess, Paulette, and Winterset	119
22	Pembroke Road and Some Actors	124
23	Australia Again	131
24	Changing Times and Equity	141
25	I Leave the Company	154
26	America and Long Day's Journey	157
27	Home Again and More Changes	160
28	The Writing on the Wall	166
Related Literature		176

Acknowledgements

A special thanks to my dear friend, Matthew Diskin, who has been our life-long friend. His devotion in getting this book published has been greatly appreciated. I would also like to thank my daughter, Brigid, who devoted hours assisting me at my home in California.

Mary-Rose McMaster
San Francisco December 2018

List of Photographs

1. Anew McMaster, aged 17
2. Anew McMaster in London, aged 20
3. Mary-Rose's mother, Marjorie Willmore (Mana) taken before the First World War
4. Anew McMaster at the height of his career
5. Anew McMaster as Othello
6. Anew McMaster as Hamlet as he appeared in the lead role at Stratford
7. Mac and Marjorie visiting Mary-Rose and Christopher at Norland Nurseries in London
8. Christopher and Mary-Rose at the Norland Nurseries (an expensive children's home run by drill sergeants)
9. Life-size portrait by the Italian artist, Gaetano De Gennaro, of Anew McMaster as Othello
10. Mary-Rose's brother, Christopher, as Fleance in *Macbeth*
11. Mary-Rose as a very unwilling Fleance in another production of *Macbeth*
12. Anew McMaster as Shylock in *The Merchant of Venice*
13. At home, 1947, sharing picnic with American film stars. Left to right: Paulette Goddard, Anew McMaster, Burgess Meredith, and Mana
14. Micheál MacLiammóir in his recital, 'The Importance of Being Oscar'. Photograph by *The Times*, London
15. Early photograph of Mary-Rose
16. Anew McMaster in *King Lear*
17. At the Dublin Theatre Festival, 1961. Left to Right: Brendan Smith; Robert Briscoe, Lord Mayor of Dublin; Mary-Rose with her late husband, Jack Aranson
18. Mac and Mana at the front door of their house in Sandymount
19. Obituary of Christopher McMaster by Christopher Fitz-Simon

Introduction

I had asked my brother Christopher to join me in a short holiday in Ireland. For many years, I had lived in California and he in England, and it seemed right that we should return together to some of the places that had 'nurtured' us as children, for the country towns of Ireland were as familiar and nostalgic to us as a beloved neighborhood might be to someone brought up in a more conventional way. Chris and I had spent our young years on tour in the classical theatre company of our father, Anew McMaster, (known to everyone as Mac) an actor with extraordinary flashes of genius. It was a life so distant from the present that it is difficult to imagine that it occurred in my lifetime and even on the same planet.

Though Christopher lived just across the Irish Sea, this would be the first time he had returned to the country in over forty years, whereas I had kept in touch as much as possible having like most 'displaced persons' an insatiable need to 'go home' where I belong. But do I belong now after more than half my life has been spent away? I suffer from the common dilemma of exiles of not quite fitting in to either place. I am still an alien in America, but to be an alien in Ireland is unthinkable and so I've clung on, leaving my family in California from time to time to 'go home.' But inevitably the changes have overtaken my occasional visits and I find myself resenting them because I wasn't there to see them evolve. I had no idea when I married in the 50s, that I would live the greater part of my life in the United States. Making plans for the future was something I had never thought about. I was young and life was endless. I was content just to let it happen. However, I had no great wish to go to America. Any regrets I may have are not that I married my husband or that I 'visited' America but that I have been away so long from the country I love.

I was to meet my brother by arrangement at the Theatre Royal in the southern port of Waterford. Our company had played at least a week there each year and we would do a nightly repertoire of perhaps *Othello, She Stoops to Conquer, An Ideal Husband, Hamlet, Ten Little Indians,* and a matinee of *Julius Caesar.* The grand old theatre was, from the outside at least, just as it was in our day – gaunt, a little decayed but beautiful, with the simple clean lines of 18th-century architecture. What memories it held, for it was here where Mrs Siddons played, and Edwin Booth and the great Henry Irving.

I arrived late, being unused to driving on the left, I had torn the side view mirror off my rented car. Chris was not there, but I recognized at once his huge slanted hand-writing on a note pinned to the main entrance of the theatre. I read that he was waiting for me in the hotel opposite.

I looked at my only brother as I entered the foyer of the hotel. He was huddled deep in an armchair, completely engrossed in whatever it was he was reading, such a familiar sight. He was rumpled and rather dirty after travelling all night by bus. But Chris always looked as though he was wearing someone else's clothes. How he looked was of no importance to him at all.

When we were both young, Chris unconsciously made me feel silly and inadequate. He was a savant: he read everything from Tiny Tots to Tolstoy at the age of seven. He read Dante's *Inferno* in Italian when he was twelve! He would read a part through once and know it perfectly. He was the bright one and I the simple minded one. And our father, who was the shining light of our family, both as an actor and as a personality, also contributed to my low self-esteem. Years later I realized that I was fairly normal – whatever that is – in a milieu of amusing and unusual people.

We decided because we had only seven or eight days to spend together that we would bypass the lush midlands, and keep instead to the more spectacular south and west. We drove to Dungarvan, to Youghal and on to the white city of Cork and down to Kinsale, Clonakilty and other towns that had been our regular touring dates, so many years ago.

The changes, particularly for Chris, were astonishing. Gone were the thin little children with matted hair and running noses and the gray houses oozing with damp. Ireland was then still suffering from the effects of centuries of British oppression. Physically defeated, but never the people, who seemed to look on their lives with amusement, as though mocking their own plight. Or perhaps they were simply accepting a condition they were powerless to change.

The towns were colourful and lovely now as Chris and I drove on stretches of brand new motorway from one remembered spot to another. There was pride in the bright well cared for gardens and the rows of newly painted houses. It was as though the country had finally come out into the spring after hundreds of years of winter. Ireland had at last 'found her place amongst the nations of the earth.' Too bad that its new found prosperity has subsequently proven to be so ethereal following the economic collapse of its much-vaunted 'Celtic Tiger' economy.

In Youghal, we found the Boat House. Did we really play *Macbeth* and *Oedipus* and *Othello* in this dilapidated old corrugated structure listing slightly sideways towards the river? Yes, and built an entire stage, complete with proscenium arch and tabs (curtains), that my mother adjusted with strings of safety pins in each town we visited.

The dressing rooms, if you could call them that, were at the opposite end of the building from the stage. We had to go outside, sometimes in the rain, tie our long Shakespearean robes around our necks, pick our way across long wet grass and mud, and up a ladder to reach the stage. I remembered the actor Pat Magee, not known for his sweet temper, muttering profanities as his boots sank further into the mud! Chris and I walked – it seemed – in the same long grass as we circumnavigated the old Boat House, and we smiled as we pictured the citizens of sunny Thebes or Cypress all splattered with mud.

We passed through the city of Cork rather quickly knowing that the beautiful old opera house where we had always played had long ago burned down. A new building had taken its place on the same site and we looked at it a little bleakly, making us aware, again, how life had continued on without us.

In Clonakilty, we bought food for lunch in a supermarket filled with marvellous varieties of merchandise; avocados, melons, cheeses from Italy, and wines from France and California. In our day, on the same site, had been a 'Medical Hall' Chris remembered as if suddenly seeing it again. 'You must remember the assistant,' he said, 'she gave away sticks of barley sugar and seemed to be 'wanting' as Mac liked to say. 'Must have been a daily communicant' I said, and we both chuckled. This was a familiar line of our father's who liked to joke about people who went to Mass every morning. Perhaps it showed to him a simple, blind faith that he secretly envied.

We went on to Skibbereen, a town that had happy memories for we usually went there in the summer and spent days swimming at the beautiful little cove called Tragumna, a few miles from the town. We arrived there late and had to stay the night above a scruffy old bar. Seedy and badly lit, we climbed the narrow creaky stairs and found two tiny rooms each with a hard little bed, a chair, and a rod strung between two boards to hang clothes. This was reminiscent of days gone by, except that the rooms, obviously partitioned to accommodate more tourists, would have been one huge one in our day, cold and bare, and smelling of mould. It was eerie somehow looking down on the narrow main street below almost unchanged. At any moment I might see Eugene Wellesley – the old character actor and a mainstay of our company – walking by in his neat suit and overcoat looking for digs perhaps. 'Getting settled', as he called it. Or, Harold Pinter (later the playwright), and Pauline Flanagan, who had become a couple almost immediately after they had met, huddling close together with heads down against the wind. More than the other towns we'd been to, Skibbereen was the least changed, and it was easy and natural to go back in time. Suddenly it was difficult to recall my present life in California. My little house perched surrounded by trees on the side of a wooded hill overlooking San Francisco's bay, my work, the people I know, and my grown-up children and grandchildren who know so little of all the years I spent travelling from one town to another. At least for the moment, I was back half a century. I would be going to the hall soon to help my mother unpack the costumes and props, and set up my place in the women's dressing room. Did I have digs this week where I would buy my own food and give it to the landlady to cook, or was it all in? Which hotel were my parents staying in? I wondered could I go there for a bath. I liked to look at the shops the first day in a new town and maybe ask the owner to keep something for me until the end of the week when I might have a little money left over after paying for my digs. How much were my digs? Thirty-five shillings! Too much!

Chris, unbelievably, was lost in Skibbereen. He had gone to buy some food and couldn't find his way back to our rather miserable accommodations, probably because he hadn't noticed where they were in the first place! For nearly an hour I searched, mostly in places that had any kind of reading material. I found him sitting on the floor of a book shop reading *A Life of Proust*. Ah, there was a change. Proust would have been unheard of and un-sellable in the Skibbereen of our day!

From 'Skib', as we called it, we drove on towards Bantry. Chris drew maps of Eastern Europe and explained the political changes taking place there at the time. I interrupted occasionally to say that I loved every one of the cows and sheep that grazed in the passing fields. I could feel Chris' gaze going heavenward as he muttered 'Oh God, here we go again.' My passion for animals was made fun of when I was young, but for a shy child who felt overwhelmed and outwitted by the clever people around me, it was natural to feel a kinship with animals. They were unthreatening, loving, and always willing to listen.

We arrived in Bantry in the wonderful glow of the setting sun. There is a timelessness about Bantry with its rows of colourful shops curving around the crescent shaped bay, hardly changed in centuries, as it seemed were the people's lives. Next day I went to Mass in the church halfway up the hill (I remembered exactly where it was), and listened to the soft tones of the old bent priest who spoke gravely about the temptations of modern life on the young. It was good to feel there are still some places left on earth almost untouched by the madness of modern life.

The smoky purple aura that sits over Bantry embraced us as we wandered about the old streets, but now we could see it with the attention of visitors. Before, we had been in a touring theatre company with all the preoccupations of setting up, finding digs, learning someone else's lines, quickly perhaps, because a member of the company had succumbed to a damp bed and had come down with the flu.

We drove through Glengarriff and into Kenmare; the name alone brings back memories of early childhood. For although we didn't generally travel with the company when we were very young, Chris and I visited our parents from time to time, and

Kenmare and Cahirciveen were two places that are particularly remembered. Perhaps it is because of some snapshots I still have of when we were three and four years old taken outside the Devonshire Arms Hotel in Kenmare, and trotting down the main street in Cahirciveen with my mother looking distracted in the background. She was, as she admitted years later, never sure what to do with small children. 'You were beyond me,' she'd say.

Kenmare sits at the entrance of the Ring of Kerry, surely one of the most wondrous places on Earth. We stopped and looked out across the exquisitely beautiful expanse of small fields, the light ever changing as the huge clouds rushed across the sky. Chris was smiling. He seemed happier than I'd known him to be in a long time. Reviving and re-treading the past (even though in later years he'd resent the years on tour), had briefly at least put aside the frustration and sadness of his present life.

For over forty years, Chris had had a successful career in Granada television in England as a writer and director of the UK's most popular and longest running 'soap', *Coronation Street*. He had married Jill Gotts, an actress in our company, and had two boys. They bought a lovely Tudor cottage in the New Forest and went to Spain and Italy in the summers. He'd loved his life, and imagined it would go on forever. When Jill divorced him and married someone else, his world crumbled to pieces. Jill had made Chris's life run like clockwork, doing all the practical things he seemed incapable of doing himself. She was as necessary as a bow to a violin, and without her he was unable to function. He lost his family, his job, his house, and for a time, his mind. In a practical sense, Chris's hold on life had always been fragile, and after two nervous breakdowns, he'd settled into a kind of limbo life and dreamed of happier times.

Chris had a special interest in Limerick, the next stop in our nostalgic wanderings, for close by was the Benedictine Priory of Glenstal Abbey where he had been to school. And well known everywhere now for their beautiful recordings of Gregorian chant. We loved playing in Limerick. The theatre was large and comfortable with 'proper' dressing rooms and a good stage where my father could indulge his passion for elaborate stage lighting. It was not often that we could unpack some of the special lamps and equipment we carried which were unusable in the smaller halls we played. Limerick was always good for business and the audiences came in droves even when there was once a transport strike. The story is still being told amongst octogenarian actors that we 'held the curtain' until the audience had been able to get to the theatre by whatever means they could. We finally 'went up' (began the play) '... well after midnight!' Greatly exaggerated, as is the retelling of most theatrical stories.

Chris liked to navigate and it was decided that we push on towards the lovely old town of Ennis situated on a narrow estuary of the Shannon River, famous for the Old Ground Hotel where our parents always stayed. The solid ivy covered building with comfortable quiet rooms and excellent food had hardly changed at all. The maids were still scurrying about in the same black dresses and white caps and aprons of the early 1950s. Silently, Chris and I drank cups of coffee. We were coming to the end of our time together. How long would it be before we'd meet again?

I had hoped that our short sojourn together in Ireland would renew his unhappy spirit – at least for a while – and it had. He was animated and funny, even optimistic, that his life would change for the better. If only a script of his would be accepted again, it would give him hope and some financial freedom.

We were full of happy nostalgia as we walked about the familiar streets of Ennis. Chris remembered a printers that was unbelievably still in business! We went in and there on the old brick wall at the back of the shop were two posters – brown and cracked – announcing the appearance at the New Theatre of 'Anew McMaster and Co. in a Repertoire of Classical and Modern Plays.' It was incredible to think that these playbills had been nailed on that same wall for over fifty years! Chris wanted to buy them but the man said casually, 'they'd been there for so many years they may as well stay another few.'

Our time was running out. We ate Chinese food without saying a word and I drove Chris to the station. He boarded the bus that would take him back to England and to the bed and breakfast where he lived in Lymington in Hampshire and I would be returning soon to my family in California, a half a world apart. I stood outside smiling and waving to him, sad to say goodbye, but relieved just a little that I would be alone again – for in the years since my own divorce I've found I enjoy my aloneness. Chris smiled too, but there was a forlorn sadness in his face. He'd always needed someone to look him, to see that his teeth were brushed and his shoes were tied and I had filled the need for a short time. But, now he looked lost again, just as he had when he was 12, and going off to begin a new term at Glenstal. I see his face every day now in my mind's eye, for it was the last time I'd ever see him.

A year went by. We had kept in touch but I could tell he was once again butting his head against a wall of disappointment and frustration. His need to write was insatiable to give his life purpose. Frantically he turned out scripts for TV. One after another, not paying enough attention to detail and it completed his despair when they were not considered for production.

I wrote to him for his birthday enclosing a little money to invite a friend to dinner to celebrate perhaps, but instead the money was used for a wreath of flowers at his funeral. He died of a massive heart attack on his 69th birthday. He had not been ill, he'd simply given up.

*****

Two years later I was back in Ireland again for a short visit. And now in Dublin, on this last day before returning to the United States, I stood solitarily looking at the elegant little Georgian house on Sandymount Strand. My parents' house; its corners slightly rounded by nearly three centuries of winters, but for all the rain and wind, I knew it would still be there long after I am gone. It was a bleak afternoon, the kind that because of the stillness and grayness made it easy to conjure the past. There were no children playing on the Strand, no little boats out for a sail, and the sea had receded so far it seemed almost possible to walk across the bay to Howth, the promontory north of the city beloved of all my family – 'My family! What family? I have no family!' To paraphrase Othello a little, 'O insupportable! O heavy hour!' O Lord, it had been instinctive for Christopher and me to continue a sentence, if it had reminded us of one, with a phrase of Shakespeare. It was not affectation, but simply part of everyday life instilled early in us as children, just as someone else might be reminded of a poem or a nursery rhyme.

I felt isolated, out of place and time. I no longer belonged to this old city that I had loved more than any other. For three days I had walked through its familiar streets, but I was invisible, a ghost from another time, a time when the Gate Theatre was bursting with energy with their stylized productions of international plays. And over at the Gaiety, my favourite of Dublin's theatres, my father and our company were likely to be doing a season of Shakespeare. They were the times when F.J. McCormick was performing his *Professor Tim* at the Abbey Theatre, a performance I have never forgotten. And Lennox Robinson was muttering Yeats to himself on the tops of buses. Later, Brendan Behan arrived on the scene like some Rabelaisian jester, and his *Borstal Boy* was discovered by the remarkable little Pike Theatre Club. They were charmed times but so is the present I'm sure for the people involved. We think of our own time, our younger days as 'the good old days', the most interesting and exciting. However, I venture to say that there is no one today like my father and Micheál Mac Liammóir, my uncle, who were extraordinary even in their own day and especially in Ireland. Expansively talented, flamboyant, theatrical and sometimes outrageous, their genre has simply ceased to be.

I wanted to walk up the little path and knock on the door of my parents' old home. I could see my father standing in the door explaining to a pair of Jehovah's Witnesses that he wasn't in the least interested in eternal life! It was easy to visualize the inside. The bedroom in the back on the ground floor, the rounded mahogany chest of drawers, the double bed with the pale green frame where my father would rest in the afternoon with a sock tied around his eyes to keep out the light and moaning – only half in jest – that life was not worth living! I could see so well the sitting room upstairs with its French 18th-century furniture of gilt and petite pointe. The gold and glass cabinet filled with Venetian glass, the little silver framed picture of my grandmother sitting on a table inlaid with mother-of-pearl, and the bright red Chinese cupboard which had belonged to the great Irish tenor, John McCormack, where my father kept the drinks. And I thought of how in lean times, he would buy the smallest possible bottle of Jameson whiskey and pour it into an antique Waterford decanter to keep up appearances 'Never let anyone know you're hard up,' he'd say, 'not good for business.'

It was in this room that my father and Micheál would have their battles of wits, each outdoing the other with exaggerated theatre stories. And it was in this ornate room that looked as if it belonged in the Petite Trianon rather than a Dublin suburb, that I first met Noel Coward who called my mother 'Little Marge' because she had hardly grown since they had acted together as children in the first production of *Peter Pan*. I remembered his valet who called him 'the master' and genuflected each time he spoke to him! I could see the pictures on the walls of the stairs of Mrs Patrick Campbell – 'Marvellous actress, absolute fiend' – my father had said of her, and his beloved Sarah Bernhardt, her eyes fixed upwards as if in private communion with some heavenly being. And there was Henry Irving in *The Bells*, and Burgess Meredith and Paulette Goddard in *Winterset*. What had become of those pictures, I wondered.

I didn't knock on the door of course, it was pleasant to daydream and I wasn't ready to awaken. I turned away and walked up the road apiece towards the Martello Tower. I wondered how it was that I was the one to be here still and my family and most of those that I worked with had 'shuffled off this mortal coil'?

All was shrouded in great gusts of gray now, the familiar houses along Sandymount Strand, the sky, the far away tide that had gone to Howth and forgotten to return leaving behind huge expanses of sand melancholy and deserted

I wandered past Christopher Casson's old house, a beloved actor who, though originally English, seemed as immovable from the Dublin theatre scene as the sand on the strand, but now inevitably he was gone too.

I felt an urgency. Something needed to be recorded before there is no one left to remember my father and a theatre long gone. It's unthinkable that he should slip into oblivion as though he'd not lived! Who should write about those times? My uncle, Micheál Mac Liammóir and my brother could have done it, both were writers, and how different their accounts would have been. Chris's clean and economical like a thesis. Micheál's dramatic, flowery, and always entertaining, and neither at all concerned with accuracy and the truth of things! Who is left to do it? I had thought of writing something for my children, but certainly not a biography. That, I'd hoped, would be done by an experienced writer with the talent and patience to research all the details of my father's professional and personal life, but so far it hasn't been done. I felt an obligation. I NEED to do it. The idea was overwhelming and frightening, but I knew I had to try.

Next day I left Ireland again and returned to my home in California to remember Mac, the most fascinating, naughty, and brilliant actor I have ever known.

1 – Birkenhead, the Early Years

Mac's background was far removed from the theatre. His father Andrew McMaster, a dour Presbyterian businessman, didn't think much of 'theatricals.' The theatre was something he had no knowledge or understanding of and certainly not to be thought of seriously as one's chief occupation.

My grandfather's forebears immigrated to Ireland from Scotland in the 17th century, and during the famine of the 1840s left Ireland to find work in England. My great-grandfather settled in Birkenhead, a suburb of Liverpool, where his son, went into 'shipping' as my father used to say rather vaguely. He was not in the hierarchy but he had a good and well paid position with the Ellerman Papayanni Line, supervising the movements of hundreds of stevedores.

I was about eight and Christopher nine when we were sent to stay with 'Gappy,' as we called our grandfather, in his big dark house in Birkenhead. I remember he was lame with gout, and kept his foot raised on a pillow and he was gruff and very strict. Chris and I kept out of his way as much as we could by 'helping' the two maids, Lotte and Lillie in the kitchen, as well as Edith the cook, who called me 'the waif' and said I looked as if I was in need of a good meal. At meals we had to keep our hands palms down on either side of our plates until we were allowed to eat. We'd take a bite and then return our hands back beside the plate again, and we would never speak until we were spoken to. On Sundays we sat in straight backed chairs and Gappy read aloud from the Bible. We couldn't laugh or sing, or listen to the radio. For recreation we were allowed to stroll for an hour around the dark lifeless shrubbery in the garden. I couldn't wait to leave and we did rather suddenly when Uncle George (my father's older brother), was sent for and Chris and I spent the rest of our 'holiday' with him, Aunt Dolly, and their four daughters. I suppose we were just too much for Gappy to deal with.

It's difficult to imagine my father in such an atmosphere. How could he have been born into a family not interested in the arts? If it is true that we choose our own parents then poor Mac must have lost his way on his journey to become mortal. Or, maybe his instinct – usually reliable – just let him down at least in the choice of his father. From the start they seemed to speak a different language. Perhaps his mother would have been his ally, but Mac had no memory of her. She died at the age of twenty-seven of tuberculosis when he was only three and a half. Her name was Alice Maude Thompson. The only photograph I ever saw of her sat in the various sitting rooms of my childhood. She was lovely, a really beautiful young woman of the period with a strong oval face, thick coils of hair, a kind, sad mouth and enormous dark eyes. It seems to me that all photographs of women at that time looked sad. Perhaps it was expected. To smile might have shown a frivolous nature. Alice's melancholy might have had something to do with knowing that her husband had one set of rules for the family, and another for himself. Gappy liked to drink –quite a lot – probably the reason for his gout. He bet on the horses and he liked the music hall and young women. I believe, though, he may have been faithful to Alice during their short marriage. When he'd been a widower for a little over a year, to everyone's surprise he married Zoe Papayanni, the daughter of a partner in the Ellerman and Papayanni Shipping Line. She was nineteen and he was forty-one. Mac was very young, but he remembered things were better and more lively at home for a time. Zoe was fun, she was dark and exotic to look at, and she played the piano well, but it all changed again when she gave birth to a baby girl, which seemed to unhinge her. All she did from then on was to play the scales from morning to night. 'Never stopped,' Mac used to say. 'All through the night too, even in the sepulchral hours before dawn, on and on and on she went.'

Of course, my father couldn't have had much memory of Zoe, but being Greek and fun must have fired his imagination and the beginnings of his love of make-believe. He delighted in telling people he was half Greek; it added colour to his life and he made up stories about Zoe's sisters, 'My Greek aunts,' he called them.

When Mac was about twelve, Gappy allowed him and Uncle George, and little sister Eileen to go to the Christmas pantomime and his imagination ran wild. For there, in a single performance, was, in various forms, almost all the performing arts – if this bizarre mixture can be thought of as art – he could be an actor, a singer, a tap dancer, a ballet dancer, a comic, an acrobat, and a magician. He could be Prince Charming or the blackest of villains! It was magic! Gappy unknowingly had opened Pandora's Box and the possibilities were boundless. Mac remembered that afternoon at the pantomime as the beginning of his life and he knew exactly what he wanted to do with it.

The theatre became Mac's greatest interest, certainly not school as most of the subjects didn't interest him and he had a way of getting out of doing anything he didn't want to do. He liked Greek and was good at it, but his interest in that was probably because if he was going to say he was half Greek, he'd better know the language! Gappy showed his disapproval in Mac's failing marks by ignoring him, and once he brought George to a matinee of *The Bells*, Henry Irving's great part on one of his farewell tours. George wasn't interested in Irving or *The Bells* and it seemed out of character for Gappy to be. It was a huge disappointment for Mac who never had another opportunity to see Irving who retired from the stage soon after.

Gappy hoped Mac would become interested in the shipping business, but he never would and any more schooling would be a waste of time and money. So when Mac was sixteen, Gappy found him a job apprenticing in a bank, but it didn't last long as Mac counted on his fingers and every transaction took so long the customers complained!

Poor Mac and poor Gappy, they were two human beings not meant to be in the same family or even in the same country. Gappy wanted a 'regular' son who could talk about ships and cricket and who knew arithmetic and didn't make up stories about being half Greek. But he did have George who did everything that was expected of him, at least until he was grown up, when the various business ventures he went into failed dismally and he kept 'touching' Gappy for more capital. In spite of this he was Gappy's favourite. He fitted into the mould and Mac didn't.

Mac happily had one ally; his mother's 'maiden' sister, Aunt Dora, known in the family as the 'brown bread aunt' because she believed in eating nothing but a particular brand of brown bread and oranges. She seemed very tall to me as a child and she wore long tube-like gray suits that made her look like a tall gray pillar. When Christopher and I went to stay in her tall gray house, she kept all the windows wide open even in the chill of the Birkenhead winter and never a heater or a fire in sight, so Chris and I crept about her frosty house in top coats and scarves. Aunt Dora was eccentric and peculiar but she did have a sensitive understanding of Mac and she seemed to be the only relative who gave him any kind of affection. Perhaps Mac's mother had a suppressed artistic nature and Aunt Dora recognized it again in him. In any case, she was sympathetic and sometimes gave him money to go to the theatre. Mac stayed in touch with her at intervals all through his life. She died at ninety-three, leaving him a little money and her narrow grey house, like a million others in the industrial cities of England.

Mac's other aunt on his father's side was Aunt Mary, 'the red nosed aunt' who lived in Warrenpoint, County Down, and from the time Mac and Uncle George were three or four years old, they spent three months there in the summer every year. Mac always looked forward to these casual months in Ireland, and Aunt Mary allowed him to get together a little theatre club and to use the carriage house at the end of the garden.

I've no memory of Aunt Mary, but from the stories I've heard she was rather a character. She suffered from 'folie de grandeur' and in her younger days thought she was too grand for any of her suitors until one day she found she had none and in her mid-forties she married a travelling salesman – in gas stoves – something she asked the family never to mention! Her red nose was not because of too much drink, apparently, but too much tea, which could not be said about her brother!

To be fair to Gappy, he probably thought he was doing his best, and strictness and discipline was part of a father's duty in the Victorian era. Besides, he was almost a bachelor father for poor Zoe had gone further into a world of her own and ended her days in an establishment for the mentally ill. It's sad that Mac never knew his own mother and had a father who didn't try to understand or know him.

Years later, when Mac was established as an actor and doing a successful season of Shakespeare in Liverpool, he invited Gappy to see *Hamlet*, but Gappy wrote back '...the sooner you realize that Shakespeare is agony for grown up people to listen to, the better.' He never saw my father on the stage and they never reconciled. Gappy died when our company was playing in Galway. I remember my mother coming in with a telegram and she said 'Mac, I'm afraid your father has died.' 'Oh, has he?' Mac said casually and that seemed to be that.

2 – London, a Mentor and a Significant Meeting

It's inevitable that anyone whose ambition is the theatre should gravitate towards London and when he was 18, off Mac went. His father made no move to stop him and he didn't give him any money either but he'd saved a small amount from the bank, enough to get himself to London and Aunt Dora provided a little more. He knew that the famous couple, Fred Terry and Julia Neilson were playing The New Theatre with their on-going production of *The Scarlet Pimpernel* and he confidently imagined he'd only have to present himself to them and be hired on the spot. Miraculously this is exactly what happened! Not as miraculous as it would be today for London before the First World War was teeming with theatre, not musicals that make up so much of the London Theatre nowadays, but drama of every kind.

Mac was engaged as a 'super' at one pound a week and he was in heaven. This was the beginning of a time that would shape his outlook and attitude towards the theatre for the rest of his life. However, a pound a week even then was not enough to live on, and after paying ten shillings for a room, he had only another ten for everything else and it didn't go far. His main meal of the day was usually a glass of milk and a bun, and he'd stay in bed until the afternoon if he wasn't rehearsing to save his energy for the evening performance. These things were unimportant. He had been awakened from his limbo life and he was learning and absorbing everything around him. He needed though to find a way to earn more money. He was losing weight from not eating properly and walking everywhere to save the tuppence on the bus; so he and another young man in the company thought of a scheme – as Mac called even the simplest of ideas; as they were both only in the first act of *The Scarlet Pimpernel*, why couldn't they 'moonlight' at another theatre and make twice the money? The Empire Theatre was very close to The New Theatre and the two were taken on in the second and third acts in the review *Everybody's Doing It*. Mac as a dancer, which seemed unlikely with his tall broad build and absolutely no training, but as he said, 'I was rather graceful you see, and I pointed my toes prettily.'

Fred Terry became Mac's mentor, an actor-manager with his roots firmly in the theatre of the 1880s and 90s; an era that greatly appealed to Mac, who seemed to have been born 30 years after his time. Terry was greatly loved as an actor and was known for his 'bell-like voice.' Aubrey Williamson in his book, *The Theatre of Two Decades*, wrote: '… only in one voice on the stage … have I heard a volume of beauty of sound to equal that which reverberated like a cathedral bell when Fred Terry spoke.' Terry had perfect diction and great charm and Mac was in his element. He learned a great deal from him, so much so that in reading more about Fred Terry myself I see such similarities between the two I felt I was reading about Mac. Not the least was Mac's own beautiful voice, becoming an actor-manager – when that era was almost over – and often preferring an earlier style of acting to the modern way.

Years later when Mac played *The Scarlet Pimpernel* himself he obviously – and wouldn't have denied it – did a complete imitation of Terry, and produced it so that he could. I can still hear him saying, 'I fear Lady Blakeney the shoe is on the other foot and pinches mightily at times, I dare swear.' His tone was conspiratorial and affected. It was hardly subtle and Mac revelled in it! He knew very well it was 'old hat' but was it really? *The Pimpernel* is set in the time of the French revolution. Naturally the characters wouldn't speak as we do now! We wouldn't say that Restoration comedy is 'old hat.' The truth of course, is that it was the style of acting of the late 19th century then still only in the recent past that was becoming old fashioned though Mac did – to his credit – 'sendup' the *Pimpernel* just a bit!

By the end of three years Mac had done his apprenticeship and was earning more money. Life was good, he had moved into a tiny flat at the top of a house and he made friendships that would last through his life. Among them was Ivor Novello, a

Welshman with an Italian sounding name who became famous as an actor, popular songwriter and composer of rather sentimental musicals; his friend Bobbie Andrews, also an actor, and the actress, Constance Collier, who was dark and beautiful in the classical style of the early 1900s and in her later years was the grande dame in many Hollywood movies.

The little circle of friends, soon to be joined by three more, were in their ways not unlike the Bloomsbury Group. They would meet usually in tea houses and endlessly discuss actors and acting, plays, opera, concerts, art exhibitions, and ideas. For my father it was a time he recalled as special and wonderful: he was young and full of enthusiasm for everything. Life seemed endless and limitless; I remember how he'd speak about those early times with a little nostalgic smile as though recalling something very beautiful and sweet.

One day in the autumn of 1912, Ivor Novello introduced my father to three young members of the *Peter Pan* company playing at His Majesty's Theatre. This was one of those chance meetings decided by fate and if it hadn't happened, all our lives would have been entirely different! One of the boys, a tall fellow with big ears and adenoids was Noël Coward, and he was playing one of the 'lost boys.' He was twelve years old and already had that air of sophisticated nonchalance for which he was famous. Later he personified a certain genre amongst people of the theatre of those days: bright, rather brittle, theatrical, not always sincere, effusive in their praise and condemnation of another actor, always entertaining and witty and very talented. I grew up knowing people like this and at the time it seemed to me that they were acting all the time. Could they stop if they wanted to? I wondered what happened to them when they were in the dark by themselves.

The other two were brother and sister; the boy was beautiful with large dark brown eyes and fair curly hair. He was smaller than Noël but exactly the same age. The girl was seventeen and seemed to be hardly there. She was shy and tiny with 'very ordinary features' as she said of herself except for a perfect nose and gorgeous long thick plaits of red-gold hair. She was there mostly to look after her brother, which she did with the gentle mixture of love and discipline of a mother. Later this unassuming girl would become my father's mainstay in every way. She was his rock, his backbone, and his alter ego, and she was of course, my mother.

The beautiful fair haired boy grew up to be Micheál Mac Liammóir with black hair and a new identity. Co-founder of the celebrated Gate Theatre in Dublin, and a multi talented man. But at this time he was still known as Alfred Willmore (his real name), and was doing very well as a boy actor. In *Peter Pan* he was Michael, and Marjorie (my mother, who liked not to be noticed), was quite happy earning her keep as the back legs of Nana, the dog.

After the run of *Peter Pan*, Noël went his worldly way, but always included Mac, Marjorie, and Micheál in his vast circle of friends. The three of them began to go everywhere together. They saw the big, heroic, biblical dramas Herbert Beerbohm Tree was famous for, which Mac loved, and the drawing room comedies George du Maurier and Charles Hawtrey made popular, which he loathed! They went to concerts at the Albert Hall with Toscanini and Stokowski conducting, and Micheál inveigled Mac to go to the ballet; a favourite of his, but not of Mac's. Best of all, Mac discovered opera with all its grandeur at Covent Garden and the three heard most of the great singers of the day: Gigli, Galli-Curci, Melba, and Caruso. Heavenly music, large choruses, full orchestra and – with luck – exquisite singing, for a man not in tune with his own time, it satisfied Mac's artistic taste completely.

I felt my mother went along more to be with Micheál and Mac than because she was particularly fascinated with any of these extraordinary artists. She would have acknowledged their greatness, but she didn't speak about them. Her responsibility and her interest then was for Micheál, and later even more so for Mac, and if something hadn't directly to do with them, it wasn't important!

There's no question London artistically must have been a very exciting place to be in these years leading up to the First World War. So much was going on in all the arts. The new style of acting; easy, casual, and realistic, 'throw-away acting', as Mac called it, was taking a firm hold. Russian opera with its magnificent singing and ornate productions were being seen for the first time, and was certainly a challenge to Covent Garden, where the singing was usually good, but the productions were dowdy and under-rehearsed. Diaghilev came with his remarkable

Ballets Russes. And the innovative new ballets of Rimski-Korsakov, Stravinski, and Borodin were danced by the greatest dancers in the world. It was the time when dozens of brilliant new writers, poets, playwrights, and artists sprung up almost as if they were all in a hurry to be recognized. I wonder does political uncertainty of the future inspire creativity more than when life is more peaceful. It's interesting that so much genius in the arts occurred just before and right after the revolution in Russia, and also before and after the war in France and Germany. And the same was true of Ireland before and after the 1916 Easter Rising. Perhaps it was just time for a new Golden Age – like the Renaissance in Italy. Mac wrote in a series of articles for *The Irish Times* that 'a golden light seems to enfold one's memories of London' (they were actually written by my mother), 'The plays we saw, the people we met, the operas we heard – it was as if we were trying to cram into life all the beauty and colour and friendship of our world.'

3 – The Willmores

My mother's family was as different from my father's as opera is to rock and roll. If they had been in another kind of work, it's unlikely my parents would have ever met, but the theatre is the equalizer that draws people together from entirely different cultures and backgrounds. It's like America in that way.

We were always much closer to my mother's family than my father's, and after that one visit to Gappy, I don't remember ever seeing him again; or Uncle George, with his droopy moustache and round eyes that reminded me of a sad sea-lion. Aunt Eileen, I never knew, but when Mac spoke of her (which was hardly at all) he made her sound a bit 'dippy' like her poor mother. 'She was difficult,' Mac would say, 'very beautiful but so difficult.'

She lived for several years with David Webster, I believe, then director of the Royal Opera House, Covent Garden, but as far as I know didn't marry him and that's all I know of her.

The Willmores were wonderful, artistic, and interesting characters; all of them. Alfred, my grandfather, was originally from Cornwall, which made him not quite English since the Cornish people are of Celtic origin. He earned a living as a miller and worked for a company that supplied grain and hay to many of the dray and carriage horses that trotted the hard streets of London every day. I was only nine years old when he died, but I still vaguely remember him as a charming, soft-spoken man with a twinkle in his eye, who created beautiful little carvings in wood. He was called 'Doc' by his family and friends because he liked to concoct home remedies for everything that didn't need surgery.

My grandmother, whom I never knew (Doc was married to his second wife, Hilda, by the time I came along), was Mary Lee. As far as I can tell she was a typical mother and housewife of the time. She cooked well, slaved over the endless laundry, and made her children's clothes. She was devoted to her family and they adored her. Mammy used to say she had a great deal to put up with and she'd cry sometimes when thinking of her.

My mother, Marjorie Helen, was the third of Alfred and Mary's four daughters and it was the youngest and the only boy Micheál, who decided that his sisters were the March girls in *Little Women*. Indeed it was astonishing how alike they were to the four sisters in Louisa May Alcott's novel. My mother couldn't have been any one but the tiny delicate Beth, though Mammy's small frame belied her extraordinary strength, which was mostly an iron will, and happily she didn't fade away early in life as poor Beth did. My beautiful Aunt Doff (Dorothy), the eldest, was the serene Meg and she was that completely. As well as being lovely to look at with gorgeous hazel eyes and thick red-gold hair, she was calm and un-dramatic and she made me feel secure and loved when I was young. Christine, free spirited and headstrong was of course the independent Jo, and the youngest, pretty scatty Peg, was the flighty Amy. Christine died mysteriously in 1934. No one ever spoke of it and Mammy would only say something evasive like: 'Christine caused my mother so much sadness.' The cause of her death was actually quite ordinary as I found out later, and the 'mystery' was probably concocted by Micheál who liked to make life more colourful than it really was.

The family lived in a small semi-detached house in the London suburb of Kensal Green and though they worked at quite ordinary jobs – like many others who lived in London – their chief interest was in the arts and the reason they were there.

My mother's interest was for literature and poetry and she read all the new young writers of the time: Rupert Brooke, Christopher Isherwood, William Faulkner, Lytton Strachey, Edith Sitwell, etc., and she loved to go to the tea houses where they gathered and listen unobserved to their ideas and philosophies by the hour. She liked the ballet, and the art museums, and she loved to draw. I still have several of her delicate pencil drawings that she did for her leaving certificate at the Slade School of Art. They reflect her stillness, her inward solitude in spite of usually being surrounded by people and her sweet Victorian delicacy. But, my mother never thought much of her own talents, and as the years went by they were submerged completely. She went on the stage only if she had to, but as Eugene Wellesley (the dear old character actor who seemed to be in our company forever) once said, 'Marjorie is marvellous, best Miss Prism in the business.' Mammy had a side to her that was very private. She used to say that she was really meant to be alone, and nothing would have pleased her more than to live in a small cottage by herself surrounded by the books she loved. But, it seems to me that we each do what we really want to do in spite of what we may say and my mother would have gone to the ends of the earth to be with my father.

Whether they knew it or not, the world of the London theatre left its mark forever on my father and Micheál, and on my mother too, but not as much. London's brand of sophistication and theatricality became part of who they were. And Micheál, in spite of an accent that an outsider might accept as being from the county Cork, his mannered style was from the same school that produced Oscar Wilde and Noel Coward (not withstanding Wilde's Dublin origin) and was more London than Dublin to me. Mac was the only one of the three who actually had Irish blood, however remote, but unlike Micheál, he didn't mind if he was thought of as an Irish actor or an English one. Politics and patriotism were unknown to him, but his outlook was definitely English, and London was the centre of the English speaking theatre for him. In the first years of his company, his actors were from England and he engaged them there. The plays he chose, besides Shakespeare, had all been successes in London at one time or another. His conversation was more about actors performing in London and the plays going on there than what was going on in Dublin. In a way he had simply transplanted his English company to the Irish provinces, however, in spite of this attitude, Ireland was where he wanted to live and work, not England. As the years went by the company was made up more and more of Irish actors.

My mother didn't seem English at all to me, but she didn't seem particularly Irish either. She belonged to that particular breed of artisan in London who fit in anywhere without seeming ethnically anything, but perhaps for that reason she was more of London than Dublin.

I should explain why being Irish or English became such an issue at all in my family: usually one is French or Italian and that's that unless one is American which can invite questions about what – usually several – ethnic background you are from. With us, it was important because of Micheál's obsession with Ireland. And as co-founder of the Dublin Gate Theatre – very talented and very visible – much has been written since his death about his 'great deception' of 'pretending to be something he was not.' Indeed, one book was not so much about his important contribution to the Irish theatre but proving his English heritage and how he managed to keep up the 'deception' with elaborate lies until his death!

Even in this day of 'expose,' far too much has been made of this deception and as everyone who knew Micheál and his talents have said 'so what?' It wasn't important to them whether he was Irish or English. For Micheál himself though, it became the most important passion of his life.

I know of no one who doesn't have a deep love of country. It's basic and primeval. But Micheál never felt it for England, and it wasn't until his first visit to Ireland as a boy when he was acting with the Herbert Beerbohm Tree Company, that he felt a sense of belonging. An affinity with the country and the beginning of a deep and everlasting need to be a part of it, not as an outsider but as an Irishman born and bred, if that could only be. It was the beginning of inventing a whole new identity for himself.

Back with his family in London, Micheál's entire focus was on Ireland and going to live there permanently one day. He immersed himself in the history, politics, the folklore, everything and anything that was Irish: he took courses at the Gaelic League and became fluent in the Irish language. His love of Ireland, its people and culture was perhaps the one completely sincere and honest emotion of his life, but he was also a child of the make-believe world of the theatre. It was not unusual at the time for actors to make up new backgrounds for themselves if it made them seem more interesting or more romantic. And for Micheál, who was a born story teller, his biography became more complicated, more detailed, and more contradictory as time went by! Still, it was not done to deceive anyone except himself. Besides, why would he want to deceive, what would have been his motive? Would it have been better for business if he was to live and work in Ireland to be thought of as being Irish? If that were so, then Hilton Edwards, Micheál's life-long partner who remained the most English of Englishmen imaginable wouldn't have become the successful actor and producer in Ireland that he did. No, it was because of a need deep within his psyche to be of the Irish race, and it was unthinkable and painful not to be. In any case, Micheál lived permanently in Ireland from the age of twenty-six until his death at seventy-eight, a lifetime. Even with his London sophistication, it was difficult to think of him as an Englishman.

From the earliest time I can remember anything, Micheál and my father were both on high pinnacles. Now with the passing of time perhaps I see things more realistically, and it's poignant to me that Micheál who had such innate good taste, understanding, and love of the Irish, as well as his talent as an actor, did not himself sound genuinely Irish; particularly when he wrote. The author of many books and plays, his last book *Enter A Goldfish*, is essentially a tale of his childhood which is half truth and half fiction where his family, from Cork, come off as sounding – dare I say it – phony. Of course, many Dubliners must have been well aware of his true background, but it just wasn't important.

Someone once said that Micheál was the only actor in the world who played a part one hundred per cent of the time all his life. How exhausting it must have been! But, I would say that I think this applied to the parts he played before he invented Micheál Mac Liammóir, or as I like to think of it, before he discovered who he really was.

4 – Mac, Mana, Micheál and the First World War

My father had been happy with the Terrys, and their influence had had a lasting effect on him, especially in his preference for the romantic theatre. He'd learned first-hand from a master actor-manager, how to be one. He had been on tour and done seasons in London usually with the two plays the Terrys were famous for, *Sweet Nell Of Old Drury* and the inevitable, *Scarlet Pimpernel,* which was always hastily resurrected when other plays flopped. Mac was beginning to play larger parts and he probably would have gone on with them until they retired, but Terry decided it was time for Mac to spread his wings, and he advised him to 'Go into the provinces my boy, get experience in melodrama, it will give you weight!' Odd advice from one who did both himself. Mac knew though, that in joining another company (and probably a less important one), that he would have more opportunity to play all kinds of parts, so he dutifully left the Terrys and joined a touring troupe to play 'as cast' and be assistant manager. Why he agreed to this I'm not sure because he was, as he said himself. 'noticeably bad at business.' He did play everything; heroes, heavies and villains. And he said years later, 'It was a tremendously valuable experience for any young actor.'

At the end of each tour, Mac always returned to London and there he'd pick up with his friends again and even continue conversations that had been left unfinished as though he'd never been away.

These years were spoken of by Mac, my mother and Micheál with the same nostalgic affection I envy a little when people speak about their university days. There were the same friendships made, the learning and exploration – and the fun.

It came to an end in 1914 when the First World War began. Mac had just been engaged to play Joseph on the tour of *Joseph and His Brethren,* a huge biblical epic produced by Beerbohm Tree and done with 'theatrical realism,' complete with flights of birds (how did they stop them from flying into the audience?) camels, sheep, horses, and goats. Mac must have been enchanted. He liked things to be done on the grand scale and he imagined that he was in for a long run, but England was not in a party mood. Theatres everywhere were playing to half-full houses, and *Joseph* dismally ended after only a few weeks. Mac, who had hardly been unemployed since his career began, was suddenly jobless. Wartime London was depressing. What to do? Suddenly, after only telling my mother and Micheál, he disappeared to Ireland to join the O'Brien Ireland, 'fit-up' company. His friends, Bobbie Andrews and Ivor Novello, thought he was demented. 'He's gone off it,' said Ivor, 'lost forever in the bogs of Ireland.' It did seem to be a curious move just as he was beginning to get a foot in on the London stage, but it was actually quite typical of him. All the large decisions in his life were made without thinking of the long-term consequences. (I've taken after him in this. I married my American husband Jack, not giving a thought of whether I really wanted to spend the greater part of my life in America, and later divorced him without any idea of how I would support my four children and myself). My father couldn't face long discussions. The easiest way was to simply act on his feelings at the time and not have to think about it at all. This time was different however, and there was a good reason for his move to Ireland. He was avoiding having to go into the armed forces. Mac could not have gone to war. He disliked violence of any kind and he was completely apolitical. Probably uppermost in his mind at the time was, where could he go to continue acting? He had no life outside the theatre and he needed to go somewhere, anywhere, so that he could remain in it. Ironically for him, radical nationalist Ireland was politically anti-conscription and was the country, whether he fully knew it or not at the time, to which he had a natural leaning to want to be there. It was all part of some haphazard structure that would finally lead him to do exactly what he wanted.

Micheál was fourteen when the war began, too young for the army and too old to go on playing boy parts. His successful career as a boy actor was over. But Micheál, unlike Mac, had many other interests and he enrolled in the Slade School of Art where my mother had gone five years before. It was time to explore his talents for painting and design.

At the Slade School, he met Máire O'Keefe, another student for whom he felt a close connection at once. 'It was as though we'd known one another for a million years,' Micheál wrote, and they grew to love each other deeply but without passion, for it wasn't in his nature to love a woman in that way. I'm not sure when I understood that Micheál was gay but I must have been well into my teens. He didn't like the new meaning for a word that means 'lively, cheerful, light-hearted' and he said to me once, 'It's sad we can't use it for that anymore.' Did I not think that Micheál's exaggerated manner and decidedly exotic appearance was different from most people? Yes, but I had always been amongst people of the theatre and most, whether gay or not, talked and behaved differently from 'ordinary' people. Micheál was just more so than anyone else. He reveled in being gay and exploited it to the hilt, and as the years went by his toupee got blacker, and his make-up thicker. At the time I was speaking of however, he was young with a head of brown curly hair, and enormous dark brown romantic eyes that could have given credibility to his imagined Spanish ancestry.

War time London had lost much of its fascination for Micheál, and after he and Máire had finished their courses at the Slade School, he decided the time was right to go to Ireland. And so together with Máire and her mother Florence (who in later years was known to us as 'Aunt Craven'), rented a cottage in Howth, the small fishing town a few miles north of Dublin that was to become 'home' to all of us, nomadic as we were. Micheál had discovered Howth as a boy and he felt an affinity for it as though he had known it, and belonged there in an earlier life. As whimsical as this may sound there is no question that Micheál, in times of stress, would always go to Howth for peace and resolution. It was home, and when he died it was quite natural that he should be buried there.

Making a living must have been difficult for Micheál during those early days in Ireland. Doc probably helped a bit, and I'm sure Aunt Craven and Máire who lived on a small fixed income provided by the mysterious and absent Mr. O'Keefe shared what they had with him. In his last book, *Enter A Goldfish*, Micheál wrote that he sold his paintings when he first arrived in Dublin, notably to the actors at the Abbey Theatre. But, as their salaries were hardly enough to live on, he couldn't have made very much! In any case, though money was scarce the three lived in a utopian world of books and painting, ideas and dreams, until Máire became ill with tuberculosis, and in 1918 they moved to Davos in Switzerland for a cure. Micheál continued to paint while looking after Máire, but quite often he managed to move freely about the continent with the ease of a man with private means. Again, in *Enter A Goldfish*, he says he sold his paintings to wealthy patrons in Monte Carlo, Switzerland, and France. His 'patrons' were likely to have been two young men he'd met in Lausanne; one American and the other English, who were happy to pay Micheál's way around Europe to be their interpreter. Micheál had an ear for languages, and if his grammar and vocabulary weren't the best, he made up for it with expressive gestures and excellent pronunciation. Of course he was more than an interpreter to both these young men – at different times I imagine – and when he'd tire of one or the other, he'd return to Aunt Craven and Máire, who like a devoted mother and sister understood and accepted his passing liaisons, and sometimes Máire even gave him sympathetic advice. She was responding well to the 'cure' and the three were making plans to go home to Howth when Máire contracted pneumonia and suddenly died. Devastated, Micheál and Aunt Craven were bound together for as long as they both lived by their mutual love for Máire. No longer in the theatre and unable to paint, Micheál had no idea what to do with the rest of his life.

With Mac in Ireland and Micheál following it might be imagined that 'Mana' as Micheál called my mother (a name I will also use since calling her Mammy at my advanced age seems a little inappropriate) was feeling rather forlorn in London during the years of the war. Not at all, she had a life now of her own that hardly included either of them – that is until she married my father.

The war had a curiously patriotic effect on my mother who wrote in her diary how she hoped a close friend, Bay Morris (who, though she never said so to me, was her first love), would 'join up' 'because we want every man available.' How English that sounds, which indeed she was, and how alien it sounds to me! She joined the war effort by becoming a draftswoman at the De Havilland Aircraft Factory, where she was given, so the story goes, her own hanger to work in because she couldn't bear the noise in the drafting room.

At weekends, my mother was sometimes invited to stay at the country houses of people who had been admirers of Micheál, and with whom she'd stayed friends after he left the stage. Mana loved the quiet of the country and the hours spent boating on the river and playing croquet, and just quietly reading. Even in wartime, the peaceful activities of the country seemed to go on undisturbed.

She met her beau, Bay Morris, through the Henry Perrins, a wealthy and conservative family who lived in Victorian luxury in Kensington, and for whom Mana first worked as a companion to Henry's maiden sister, Emily. Bay was the brother of Henry's daughter-in-law Susan. 'Daddy Perrin,' as Chris and I later called him, was a lovely gentle soul; tall and elegant with a grey beard. He looked like an older Nicholas of Russia and I remember wishing that Gappy could have been more like him. The Perrins and my mother stayed friends all their lives and Bay, at the time, her special one.

Mana never talked about Bay, but I can tell from the very scanty entries in her diaries that he was special to her. She wrote simply 'Had tea with Bay today,' and 'Met Bay at Victoria Station.' Her entries became anxious when he'd been away at the war and she'd write, 'No word from Bay, if only he'd write.' And when he'd reappear she wrote, 'Spent the day with Bay, picnic at Hampton Court.' Bay was killed in France in 1916, and no more was written. Mana was close to 'Aunt' Emily and 'Aunt' Sue – Bay's sister – whose husband Maurice also died in the war leaving her with a baby on the way. Many years later her daughter joined our company as an apprentice. She was very pretty I recall, but the theatre was just a passing fad and she 'retired' when she was twenty or so and never did another day's work in her life.

Another interest of my mother's was the right of women to vote movement. She and Aunt Emily joined the suffragettes and marched in the streets waving flags and shouting slogans. They were quite militant – for a short time – for though Mana had strong convictions, it was not in her character, or Aunt Emily's, to be so aggressive.

After Micheál, Máire and Aunt Craven (such an abundance of aunts!) went to live in Ireland, Mana occasionally visited them, but she hardly saw anything of Mac who stayed in Ireland during the four years of the war.

5 – Vanished to Australia

Everything seemed to happen to my father for a reason and the years spent in Ireland with the fit-up company were all part of a jigsaw puzzle Mac was doing unknowingly, and the pieces were all fitting perfectly together one by one. The O'Brien fit-up company in Ireland was a group of players who had done it for years. There was nothing they didn't know about the business of touring, and Mac learned everything about it from them, though he had no thought at the time of forming his own company.

By 1918 when the war had ended Mac's only thought was to get back to London and into the swing of things again. But he came back to a very different theatre. Gone were the epics of Beerbohm Tree. His mentors, the Terrys, had retired. The 'Grand Manner' was out and the 'cup and saucer' school was in, and audiences were more interested in the playwright and who the director was than the actors. Mac must have felt that 'time was out of joint' for him, but he adapted well and landed the second lead in a light comedy called *Paddy The Next Best Thing*. The play had had a big success in New York and it was headed for the West End after a provincial tour. It opened in London early in 1920, and was a huge success. Mac was in for a long run.

He moved into a comfortable little flat where he was able to invite his friends instead of meeting as he'd always done at Lyons Corner House, or Appenrodt's, a delicatessen near Oxford Circus. Mana often visited and Mac began to depend on her for all the practical things he wasn't good at, and their affection for each other grew. But Mana never talked about the probability that she and my father were becoming more than 'just friends'. For her it was almost as if such a thing would be 'unsavoury,' and any mention of sex, especially if it involved them, was taboo (Mac was quite the opposite, he delighted in jokes about sex and sexual scandal.) Perhaps this is what she wanted to convey to Chris and me because children weren't supposed to know about such things. In any case, she seemed to think she was unworthy of Mac, for what would this gorgeous creature be doing with 'Little Mouse', as some of her friends called her. She always disparaged the way she looked, saying things like 'my mouth is too big, and my body is too small.' Actually, she was perfectly proportioned and she had the most perfect nose I have ever seen.

Mac had had good reviews and he settled in for a long run. Heaven for most actors, but for Mac, the repetition of doing what to him was a frothy bit of nonsense was deadly, and after a year, he'd reached 'screaming point'. He had to leave. By coincidence, R.M. Williamson, an Australian producer, was in London looking for actors and saw Mac's performance and after talking to him, Williamson asked the management of *Paddy* to release him from his contract, which was done and Mac was free to escape.

Mac left London as suddenly as he'd left for Ireland and again his friends thought he'd 'gone off it.' Mana was in Ireland at the time visiting Micheál and Máire, and Mac wrote to her; 'Darling Marjorie. By the time you get this, I'll be on my way to Australia. I don't know why I'm going but there was no one to tell me not to. I'll write someday. Love to Micheál and yourself. Mac.' How typical this was of my father. No thought of what his absence would do to his future as a London actor. Life had become predictable and routine, he needed an adventure and he leaped at the first opportunity to get away. Australia was thought of as being behind the times in those days, at least theatrically, and I'm sure Mac hoped he'd be playing some meaty parts in some good old-fashioned plays. He had no idea until he was handed the script on board ship that the first play he was to be in was *Paddy the Next Best Thing*!

The play opened in Sydney and was a hit, but Mac was disenchanted. He could see himself being stuck again. Nothing had really changed except he was doing it in 100 degree weather instead of the greyness of London. He was homesick too, and he asked the Williamson management to let him out of his contract, but they enticed him to stay with the promise of more interesting parts, and more money, so he did. Everything in Mac's life, whether he was happy or unhappy, had to do entirely with what he was doing in the theatre at the time, and over the next six months he did play parts that were more satisfying, and so Sydney suddenly became a pleasant place to be.

He enjoyed the outdoor life, the surfing and swimming the only sport he really enjoyed, and he liked to tell the tale of how he was bitten by a shark off Bondi Beach, 'Made a gash in me arm as big as a crater, dear.' And it was true, to a degree, because he kept a newspaper with the heading; 'Irish actor's lucky escape from shark.' He didn't miss a performance though, so the 'gash' was probably no more than a scratch. However, in spite of the pleasures and the relative ease of his life and work, he was aching to get back to London. He wasn't happy being alone; he didn't have anyone close to help him make decisions and look after him. He missed Mana and wrote how he couldn't wait to leave but each time his six-month contract expired it was renewed with the enticement of more money. Mac would usually not have stayed anywhere if he hadn't wanted to. Money was never a reason for doing anything he didn't want to do, but once again his instinct must have motivated him to stay, for if he had gone home, it's likely that he'd never have met Oscar Asche, who became the third big influence in his life, after Henry Irving and Fred Terry.

Oscar Asche was an Australian actor-manager who had had his training and experience in England where he was well known for his 'robust' productions of melodrama and Shakespeare. He was also robust. A gigantic man, with a deep booming voice and his heart was in the old tradition of romantic theatre as much as Mac's. Asche was back in Australia to do a season at the Theatre Royal in Sydney and Mac, knowing of his reputation, was keen to work with him. He presented himself to Asche one afternoon who invited him, on the spot, to play in *Iris* by Arthur Wing Pinero. He told Mac that he was going to produce *The Taming of the Shrew* and *Othello* for which he was famous – if he could find the right Iago. Mac had done no Shakespeare yet, and was dying to. So, with more wile than he generally used, or knew he had, he told Asche that he would play in *Iris* with him if he could play Iago. Asche, to Mac's great surprise agreed.

Mac was naturally 'excited beyond words,' but now he had to learn one of the longest parts ever written, and Mac was a rotten student. It was truly agony for him to learn lines (and one of the reasons that he was content to repeat many of the same parts over and over when he had his own company). At the dress rehearsal of *Othello*, Mac was far from 'word perfect,' but Oscar didn't seem discouraged and he told him to take a drive into the country and not to look at his words again. Mac, who rather liked a voice of authority telling him what he should do, did what he was told and it worked – almost. *Othello* was a great success and Mac had some good – and a few not so good – reviews. One critic wrote: 'Mr. McMaster was brilliant in the temptation scene and ... deservedly shared in the tumultuous applause at the end.' But, the same critic also wrote that he was 'at times overdoing it, which he hoped the actor would reduce with experience.' This was something Mac would do when he wasn't sure of the lines. I could always tell, there was no hesitation or apparent nervousness, but he'd 'pong it' to use his own expression, or press on it.

After *The Taming of the Shrew*, which was described by a critic as 'a breathless, knockabout, rampageous show,' Oscar put on *The Spanish Main*, a swashbuckling adventure tale written by him. Oscar naturally cast himself as the dashing young hero, swinging – all 400 lbs. of him – like a pendulum between two precariously bending masts! Mac, tall, handsome, and blond was cast as the black-hearted villain, Pedro Malorix, the vulture. Well, at least he was playing some juicy parts and he would be forever grateful to Oscar for giving him his first opportunity to play Shakespeare. However, with all his success and money, Mac's homesickness prevailed.

By 1924, Mac had been in Australia almost three years. He'd liked a lot about it. It was 'innocent', as he said. The people, even if their vowel sounds weren't the best, were straightforward and uncomplicated. He was fascinated by the timelessness and vastness of the Outback and he had made some good friends. But it was time to go home, and he wrote to Mana to say that he had finally been able to make the break and was on his way. Mac's letters to my mother had been spasmodic and short and they came straight to the point. In his last before leaving, he wrote: 'My dear Marjorie, I love you more and more with each passing minute I am away from you, with some people it's not that way, is it? I can't be, in the long run, as rotten and changeable as I think I am. Mac.'

Mac sailed away from the Antipodes – his pockets bulging with travellers checks. He loved spending money and often bought things just for the thrill of buying. Mana called it 'squandermania' and to compensate for the boredom of being on board ship which he found excruciating, he'd go on spending sprees in every port the ship docked in. He bought whole bolts of silks, damasks, and velvets and all kinds of jewellery. I'm not sure he knew himself what to do with them. They seemed superfluous at the time.

Mac decided to leave the ship in Naples and cabled Micheál, who was in Switzerland, to meet him for a holiday. They had not seen each other for over three years and Micheál wrote that Mac hadn't changed a bit except for 'an air of opulence,' and having 'a vast array of jewels and gold cigarette cases. These were the alterations I could trace. Inwardly he was, as he had always been, at a mysteriously pitched-up key of perpetual excitement and high spirits.'

In Italy, Mac's 'squandermania' reached the point of over indulgence as he bought Venetian glass, tapestries, replicas of the Renaissance and a real della Robbia as I always thought it was, but surely if it had been genuine, it would have been a priceless treasure.

The two parted in Florence, Micheál returning to Switzerland and Mac eventually arriving in London, via Paris. He had cabled my mother before leaving asking her to find him a flat, and she had – a big airy one in Portman Square.

6 – An Arabian Prince Returns, and 'Iris'

In London, Mac arrived at the flat like a visiting Arabian prince with wardrobe trunks, crates, and huge packing cases 'crammed into five taxis,' so my mother once wrote, but she was tainted with the family weakness for exaggeration. Mícheál and Mac did it to make a story funnier or more interesting; Mana to emphasize something. Chris and I did it because it was the best way we knew of getting attention.

Mac was on top of the world. He was actually home again and amongst his closest friends. He didn't have to worry about money for the present, and the expectation of what was around the corner in the theatre was exhilarating. Then came the episode of the black carpet, the cleaners, and why my parents decided to get married.

Before Mac came home, my mother had brought a black carpet of his to the cleaners and gave her name of Willmore to the clerk. So when Mac went to pick it up, the clerk wouldn't give it to him because he didn't have the receipt and his was the wrong name. When Mana began to explain, Mac stopped her and in a series of articles for *The Irish Times*, she wrote: 'Still shaving and with his face twisted into the most unnatural shapes, he hissed through the corner of his mouth, 'You know, Marjorie, to avoid all this sort of confusion, why not let's get married, then there'd be only one name between us?' I said that I didn't see why I should get married over a black carpet! Then, he suddenly turned his enormous blue eyes on me and feeling for the spots on his face the razor had missed, he said, 'You see anyway I told my Chinese dresser in Australia that we were getting married when I came back from Europe.' He seemed to think that had settled it, and it had. There she was playing down again that she and Mac were becoming closer. Did she feel awkward that their long platonic friendship had blossomed into something else? Perhaps more embarrassing was that it really hadn't, yet. It was still more of a mutual need, a feeling of being completely comfortable with one another. Mac too, was probably a little embarrassed, he wasn't known for his conquests of women and most of his friends were male. In any case, he told no one, and Mana too kept it secret, not telling her parents, her sisters, or even Micheál. On 27 July 1924, they were married at Marylebone Registrar's Office, with four witnesses; Mac's brother George, his favourite Aunt Dora, Mana's friend Sue Perrin, and Bobbie Andrews, the only theatre friend present. Once again, Mac had instinctively done exactly the right thing for his future by marrying Mana.

Now he was back from his 'triumphs' in Australia, his goal was to get back to the West End, do some good parts in worthwhile plays and live the life of a successful London actor. He'd been out of sight for a long time and he knew it might be difficult.

As luck would have it, Oscar Asche was back in London to do a French play called *Le Roi,* and cast Mac in a small, but showy part. Lots of money was spent on the production, but it flopped and ended after only nine performances. Next he heard that John Barrymore was in London to produce his famous *Hamlet*. Mac was full of excitement and he hoped that Constance Collier, his old friend, who was to play Gertrude, would introduce him to Barrymore, but he decided against it. Instead he chose to try for *Iris*, the play in which he'd played Laurence Trenwith in Australia, and about to be produced by Gerald du Maurier. To play it again in the West End would do more to establish him as a leading man than playing a minor part in *Hamlet*. The decision must have been a difficult one and I'm sure was my mother's; Mac would have done what he wanted rather than what was best for his career. He auditioned and got the part of Trenwith in *Iris* and, to celebrate, Mac and Mana took off for a holiday in France, where as Ivor remarked, 'There must be more to it (their marriage) than one is led to believe,' because Christopher was conceived there. The mutual and practical need they had had for one another, had travelled rather quickly to romantic love. From then on Mana's love for my father absorbed her completely.

Iris was to star the beautiful and popular Gladys Cooper, a name synonymous with the devil in the family as I was growing up. She had the reputation for being difficult and Mac felt waves of dissention emanating from her from the start, probably because she had wanted Ivor Novello to play the part, but he was making a film and she had settled reluctantly for Mac. Trouble began almost at once, she made it impossible for him to play love scenes, turning her face away when he tried to kiss her and keeping her hat and gloves on and reading from the script right up to the dress rehearsal. Sometimes she would have private conversations with Gerald du Maurier behind closed doors, which Mac imagined were about him. Most undermining was that she was critical of the way Mac was playing the part. She was of the new 'cup and saucer' style of acting where lines were mumbled or 'thrown away.' Mac was not. In Australia he had played the part in what must had been quite a different production and Oscar was a large actor in every sense of the word and was probably more suited to the villain Mouldonado than Henry Ainley who, as *The Daily Sketch* said: '... was so handsome, so attractive and his glorious voice rang out so passionately that one wanted to tell Iris not to be so peevish and marry him right away.' (In the play, Iris wavers between marrying the villain for his money, or the virtuous and handsome Trenwith.) Another critic wrote: '(Ainley's) Mouldonado was so much more distinguished than the Laurence Trenwith that one could hardly sympathize with Iris.' Criticism is difficult for any actor, but most have more steel in their backbone to deal with it better than my father and most have other talents as well as acting to interest them. Mac had only one interest and one talent, everything else was unknown except in passing and when this only thing he knew he did well was attacked, he felt stripped. It undermined him completely, and he felt shame and humiliation as if something in his personal make-up was not right.

The play was dated, and with mixed reviews, something had to be done to boost the box-office and Gladys Cooper had no intention of being in a flop. It would damage her aura and her future. Then Mac heard whispers that a name was to be brought in to replace him to save the play and – more humiliation – whispers that his close friend, Ivor Novello, who was now free, would be playing the part. The rumours turned out to be true. My mother, like a wild animal protecting her young was outraged at what she felt was Ivor's treachery. Mac, mortally wounded was silent, it wasn't in his nature to fight back, he just wanted to disappear – and he did.

He would escape to Ireland. The decision was made just as much on the spur of the moment as his previous 'disappearances'. In various articles and interviews he said that it had always been in the back of his mind to form his own classical company in Ireland, and perhaps deep in his subconscious was an idea, unformed and certainly not thought of as a practical reality for the immediate future. Perhaps buying those rich materials en route from Australia was because he knew that one day they would be used for costumes in his own company. One day came sooner than expected. He felt he had to leave London, and Ireland was the obvious country. It was English speaking, he was naturally drawn to it, he'd had four years of touring there before, and he knew the ropes. He loved the people who had a natural appreciation for good drama and the spoken word. If it had been a dream it would not have been surprising, but until the *Iris* episode, London was where he'd expected to continue his life and career. Mac's decision was so swift that even my mother was taken by surprise and she wrote in her appointment diary: 'Spent the day sorting out clothes and packing for our going away – but where? Mac, too miserable about coming out of the play to stay here.' When she did know, she wasn't at all sure it was the right thing to do. She would have been happier for Mac to show a little more toughness and eventually rebound as good as new, but she knew him better than anyone and though she guided him, guarded him against 'the slings and arrows', and goaded him when he needed a push, she knew very well that the big life-changing decisions could only be made by him. His guardian angel would always make the right decisions for him and that meant for her, too, though sometimes at the time they seemed to make no sense at all.

I believe the move to Ireland was inevitable, it just happened sooner in Mac's life than it could have. With his heart and talent in an earlier time, the writing was on the wall for him to go on working in London. It may have been possible for him to have adapted to the changing styles but he simply didn't want to and he wouldn't have been happy. Besides, all the experiences he had had so far seemed to be groundwork for what would turn out to be his life's work. It was predestined.

7 – Flight into Ireland

Mac rushed over to Ireland to make some preliminary arrangements for the first tour. Micheál, who was living in Ireland, had no idea of Mac's plans until they were together one day on the Hill of Howth. As Micheál wrote in his later autobiography *All For Hecuba*, Mac announced:

> I've turned on it (London) forever. It's a rat race, and now I'm going to take out my own tour of Shakespeare. We'll begin with *Hamlet, Romeo,* and *The Merchant* ... others later on, *Macbeth* and *Richard III*, and perhaps later some of the Greek tragedies.

He hissed suddenly:

> Fit-ups with a black velvet background and great splashes of colour, marvellous dresses ... and possibly some small insets, and I'm going to spend every bloody sou I've earned on a light plant. One can do so much with light. Imagine it; jewels glowing on a black velvet background ... and Shakespeare's words, what do you think of that?

'Superb, but where? I mean where do you mean to do it?'
'Here in Ireland of course ... towns like Dungarvan and Skibbereen ... their taste has never been spoiled you see. They've hardly seen a film even. They've seen nothing for years but *No Mother to Guide Her,* or *Waifs and Stray's on Erin's Isle.*'
'Then will they ever ...?'
'Come to Shakespeare? Yes, they will and that's why, because they're pure you see ... I've made enough to start off with, and all I ask of Ireland is a living. Just a living, dear.'

Mana had stayed in London and was up to her eyes with the organization and gathering of everything needed for the first tour, and all in a few weeks, for she knew that to save Mac from deep depression, which in spite of his usually 'sunny disposition' was always just below the surface, it all had to be done as rapidly as possible. As Mac (really Mana) later described the scene in the series of articles for *The Irish Times*:

> Our flat took on a new aspect, big boxes began to pile up on chairs, bales of materials and pyramids of shoes, lights, swords and daggers smothered the beds and couches and the hall was filled with brand new hampers bearing the inscription 'McMaster Shakespeare Co.'

Two of these hampers, worn down after over thirty years of touring and containing many of the Shakespeare costumes, arrived at my little house in California a few months after my mother died. They seem so out of place here and I feel sad for them for once they were resplendent and much admired, and now they are incarcerated and left to decay like so many bodies in their graves. Once a year I take them out to 'air' them only to be put back for another year. What to do with them? The rich velvets, silks, leathers and furs are all looking sad and faded now, but I cannot discard them. They are the only tangible relics I have of a time long gone.

Most of the new company of actors had been interviewed and engaged by Bobbie Andrews, and he cast them and rehearsed them at Mac's request, and in less than five weeks, a new theatre company had been formed with most of the actors, and all the scenery, costumes, props and lighting needed. The first six weeks of towns were booked and the publicity was out, it was an enormous undertaking organized entirely by my mother who didn't seem at all concerned that she was by this time five months pregnant. She told no one and kept it secret by wearing a very large camouflaging fur coat. It was not the most convenient time to be pregnant and Mac was the important one, not her, even to herself. She wanted to ignore her condition as long as she could. The only concession made to my dearest brother was that the first tour would be short, so that she could go back to London where her doctor was, when her time came to have the baby.

London was still the place to go back to and it was decided to keep the flat on in spite of Mac's ultimatum that he had turned against it forever. It was home, and as well, they weren't absolutely sure how the first tour would do. Mac felt reasonably sure that the audiences in the smaller towns who had probably never seen Shakespeare would lap it up. It would appeal to their senses, the humour, the dramatic situations, the beautiful costumes, and the mysteriously changing lighting effects. 'They were,' as Micheál wrote: 'so simple that they could understand him [Shakespeare] if not profoundly at least with passion.' These were the people that Mac wanted to reach, not the intellectuals, who approved 'more with their heads than their hearts,' as he once wrote.

Mac in his more sophisticated way was not unlike the country audiences, he had little use for those who needed to dig deep into the psychological make-up of a character which he found boring and unnecessary. Yes, his approach was un-intellectual, but it worked for him because his instincts and emotions were usually inspired.

The first repertoire would be small, only four plays, three of them by Shakespeare: *Hamlet, The Merchant of Venice, Othello*, and *Trilby*, the melodrama by George du Maurier about a girl who is hypnotized by Svengali, an evil and domineering man, into singing like an angel and she becomes a famous concert artist. The inevitable happens, when he is not there fixing her with his terrifying stare, she is unable to sing a note and is booed off the stage. It's a marvellous showy part for any actor and I can still see my father in it as if it was yesterday. The black oily hair almost to his shoulders, the pointed black beard, his eyes menacing and very bright, as he plays Schubert's *Rosamunde* with great flourishes on the piano, I can still hear his voice insinuating and sinister as he's putting Trilby into a trance, 'You will speak of nothing, hear nothing, think of nothing, but Svengali, Svengali, Svengali'. Who wouldn't want to play a part like that? Didn't John Barrymore do the same as Rasputin?

In those days, actors, especially actor-managers, often put on plays that were mediocre, sometimes downright bad if they had a plum part that they couldn't resist! Irving did it with *The Bells* and Mac's old mentor Fred Terry did it with *The Scarlet Pimpernel*. Mac with his own company could indulge himself as much as he liked and he did with plays like *The Speckled Band* and *Mr. Wu*. Not to be taken too seriously by Mac or the audience. But they were entertaining and fun.

Mac was still under contract with the *Iris* Company when he began the first tour and he wasn't supposed to act with his or any other company until it expired, but he did, and changed his name to Martin Doran, not to be tracked down. He probably felt a little satisfaction in defying the *Iris* management too. Mana wrote that he was in high spirits about the establishment of his new company and she hoped that the *Iris* episode was being forgotten and to a degree it was, but the damaging effect it had on his psyche always stayed with him. Publicly he saved face by saying that he and the leading lady hadn't seen eye to eye artistically and it had been his decision to leave the cast and that it had actually been a blessing in disguise because it cleared the way for him to 'realize his dream of doing the classics in Ireland.' At home though, whenever Gladys Cooper's name was mentioned, Mac would turn a pale shade of green and mumble something like, 'I hope she rots half a grain a day, the bloody cow!' In time his dislike for her seemed to become more exaggerated, which was done rather more for theatrical effect than an ongoing grudge. If he saw her on the screen, for instance, he'd stifle a sound of annoyance and say in a loud stage whisper, 'The unmitigated bitch and people say she's beautiful, ha!'

8 -The First Tours and Micheál and Hilton

I can find no account of the first tour. Mana's brief entries in her diaries give no information other than 'Open Wicklow, good house,' and later in another town she wrote; 'Good audience, lousy hall.' In September when the tour ended Mana wrote simply: 'Exhausted.' She was, completely, and she and Mac returned to London to rest and get ready for Christopher's birth which she knew might be difficult being as tiny as she was. Mac, usually so willing to be led by my mother, showed quite a different side to his nature in the times when she needed him. He took control and he was more than usually attentive and loving towards her, but towards others like a little boy whose security is threatened when his mother is ill. It frightened him, and he took on a steeliness that seemed out of character. Mac had insisted that Mana be under the care of the most eminent – and expensive – gynaecologist in London, Mr. Simpson, who less than a year later delivered the Duchess of York's first child, Princess Elizabeth. He reserved a room in an exclusive private nursing home, in spite of Mana's protests, and she went to stay there three weeks before the date Christopher was due. On November 3rd, 1925, Christopher was delivered by caesarean section, a procedure, though spoken of by Shakespeare, that was still risky at that time.

Mana seemed quite nonchalant about the whole thing and the five little words in her appointment diary say nothing about her state of mind: 'Baby born 9:20. John Christopher.' Nothing more! Was she excited? Relieved? Anxious? Worried? Happy? No more until November 16th when she wrote: 'Specialist to see baby,' and that's all there is! It was after all an appointment diary not a journal, but how could she have resisted saying more about this milestone in her life? It seems odd too that she kept a diary not to remind her to keep appointments, but to jot them down after they had happened, as: 'Had tea with Bobbie (Andrews)' and 'Went to see Emily (Perrin).' Chris's birth seemed to have no more importance than this.

What was important at the time was the building and sustaining of a brand new theatre company. It was a time of trial and error and lots of hard work and whatever was in her heart, Mana made the choice of being Mac's backbone in all things, rather than being a mother, it wasn't possible to be both, and when Chris was a month old she left him in the care of the Norland Nurseries in London, a formidable fortress of a place run on a strict and unwavering schedule by a team of drill sergeants disguised as nannies. Poor Chris, though everything was done very properly for him physically, I believe he suffered from a kind of emotional isolation there. In later life it was difficult for him to really connect with people closely, even his wife, and he lost himself in his own quiet world of non-stop reading, map drawing, and accumulating thousands of historical facts. He was insulating himself from a society he didn't feel at home in.

By the time Mana saw Chris again she was almost seven months pregnant with me. I'm not sure if she planned this, feeling perhaps that Chris should have a playmate, or as is more likely in those days, it just happened. What Mac thought about being a parent can only be imagined. It would be fun occasionally to have two little buddies to play with. The making of decisions and responsibility for us would be someone else's business, Mana's of course, and I'm sure he thought of plays that would have nice showy parts for two children.

The first tour had been encouraging enough for Mac and Mana to feel that it could be a permanent way of life for them, and that they should do it on a larger scale. The first company had been fairly small and included some experienced middle-aged actors who were not looking for stardom in the West End and were content to be working and playing worthwhile parts. These actors, strong and reliable, were the backbone of the company and they stayed with the company for several years. The younger ones would come and go, but there was always plenty to choose from. Acting schools were not the prerequisite they seem to be today, and many preferred to get their experience by apprenticing with repertory and touring companies, and my father's company specializing in Shakespeare would become a recognized training ground for young actors. Mac stuck to his original idea of a minimum of scenery done out of practical necessity rather than any great innovation on his part, but with the beautiful costumes and intricate lighting effects Mac was very much an innovator. No one in rural Ireland had seen anything like them. I remember especially the 18th century costumes for plays like *School for Scandal* and *David Garrick*. They were exquisite and made from the richest brocades, velvets, and slipper satins, and sewn with rhinestones and pearls. Mana didn't like such extravagance and said the same effect could be had with upholstery and curtain materials, but Mac wanted the audience to be dazzled. Sadly, these costumes were lost in a fire in Donegal, they were never replaced and the 18th century plays were dropped from the repertoire.

The second tour opened in Athlone in the midlands and although it was known in later years for having a thriving dramatic society, at this time the citizens were not particularly interested in Mac or his company and the houses were woefully small. Mac took to the streets and with bell, book and candle he dramatically denounced the town for their lack of taste. Thank goodness the people thought it was great fun and some even joined in the march.

These beginning tours were all a time of learning for Mac, he hadn't had much experience with Shakespeare's plays yet, and here he was directing and acting in four of them, but he was entirely in his element. It was what he was born to do.

The company expanded, more plays were added, and especially more of Mac's mania for the newest and most expensive in lighting equipment. The basic sets would always remain, which for Shakespeare consisted of the 'old men' which were enormous hessian drapes painted with elderly men of the Renaissance in rich costumes used for interior scenes, the cyclorama, rostrums, and cut-out pieces that suggested the locale for the outdoors. It was practical and effective and it eliminated long waits between scenes. The company carried one box set for the more modern plays. It was interchangeable and even used back to front. Through the years my mother painted it and repainted it. It was amazing how different it could look with different props and pictures and curtains on the windows. The same basic set was used for a cottage in *The Bells*, and for the elegant drawing room in *Lady Windermere's Fan*.

About half way through the second tour came the time for me – and rather inconveniently – to be born and my mother swathed in the same long bulky fur coat she had worn before to hide her condition, discreetly left the company on her own and travelled to Dublin where, on November 10th, a year and a week after Christopher's birth, I was delivered by caesarean section at Hatch Street Nursing Home, giving me the distinction of being the only member of my family to be born in Ireland. That is until my own daughter was born at the Rotunda in Dublin some 30 years later. I came into the world tentatively, undecided whether I really wanted to stay, undersized with 'dark stringy hair'. I was too feeble to draw milk from a bottle and was fed, so the story goes, with drops from a fountain pen filler. Poor Mana, she had enough on her plate without having to worry about me. She knew she was indispensable to Mac, so she left me in the hands of professionals and, as soon as she was strong enough, went back on tour where 'Nobody had the slightest idea that I had had you, or that I'd even been pregnant,' she told me in later years.

At the time, both Christopher and I were complications that could have been done without. The time was out of joint. A few years later perhaps when the company was firmly established, I'm sure Mana would have taken time away to be a mother. As it was, she missed a very important time, the first few months of life, the days and nights of closeness and concern when an unbreakable bond is made, and out of it comes the special unconditional love that only exists between a mother and child. My little mother deprived herself of this and it can't be regained. She loved us I have no doubt of that, but it was an impersonal kind of love, un-maternal and at arms' length. Her devotion to my father consumed her, she knew it and she said to Chris and me when we were grown, that she should never have been a mother because she didn't have the natural instincts. I poo-pooed the idea and told her that I loved her, and I did.

In the spring of 1927, when I was about five months old, I joined Chris and the drill sergeants at the Norland Nurseries. A new tour was about to take off and as usual new actors were engaged and rehearsed in London and though rural Ireland was thought of then as a sort of theatrical back-wash, Mac was getting the reputation for doing good plays well and he attracted some of the best. Amongst these was David Gill, son of the well-known actor, Basil Gill, and I remember him being there on and off throughout my childhood. He was attractive, experienced and cast to play some important parts like Iago, Bassanio and the King in *Hamlet*. Another was Bovay Parry, a regular at Stratford and in need of a little adventure, and Ian Priestly-Mitchell, a little man with an oily insinuating manner like Uriah Heap. The women included Esme Biddle, a tall blond English girl, whose serene patrician features and cultivated manner hid her secret weakness for the drink. Coralie Carmichael, dark and dramatic and 'born to play Clytemnestra' Micheál later remarked, and pretty Anne Clark, the ingénue. As Carl Falb, an American student who wrote his thesis on Mac, said: 'The company was remarkably distinguished for a young touring group.' Micheál who was still wandering in France and Italy also joined the company at this time and in a letter to Mac in *All for Hecuba*, he wrote, 'My dear Mac, now that Máire is no more, I find it impossible to go on with the old life. (Herbert Beerbohm) Tree used to think I could act and gave me all the boy parts he could find. You were of the same opinion, or said you were. Could you give me any work? I've forgotten much and feel in worse condition than a real beginner because I'm conscious of the depths beneath my feet … Mac replied in a series of telegrams and letters each contradicting the last.' (Ten days later or so, Micheál joined the company rehearsing in London.) 'My years as a boy actor only served to mock me.' Micheál continued dramatically, 'All that I'd learned from Tree and from Dion Boucicault had vanished.' I doubt that he really believed this himself. He often wrote for dramatic effect, and he never lacked self-confidence. Even when he'd look someone straight in the eye and tell them a completely made up story, he did it with such conviction that no one thought to question it!

Mac told him not to worry, that 'warm oil would start the engine turning again', and it did. He fitted in like an old pro at rehearsals and quickly made friends with the other actors, particularly with Coralie Carmichael who had reminded him of Clytemnestra. She later joined his Gate Theatre Company and stayed with it until her death 30 or so years later.

At the end of a frenetic rehearsal period in London, the company gathered at Euston Station for the now usual crossing to Ireland. Micheál remembers everyone being in good spirits. It was late spring, a glorious time, and for the several new people it was an adventure to be doing Shakespeare in a country they had not been to before and for the others it was good to be working again with actors who had become close friends. The train was about to pull out, and Mac and my mother arrived late in a state of anxiety, at least Mac was. My mother was usually calm in times of crisis, and it was a minor crisis because David Gill was not coming! Micheál wrote in *All For Hecuba*, 'We've been let down, shouted Mac through the whistles and screeching steam of the engine, has a problem with the bottle, better off without him, but now we have to stay here to find a replacement, we'll join you as soon as we've found him.' And off they disappeared into billows of steam. The company, now feeling rather unsettled, continued on to Enniscorthy. For the next several days they rehearsed with Micheál in charge, who in spite of his professed misgivings was probably wondering by now why he'd spent so much time in aimless wandering when he could have been acting all the time.

About the fourth day, my parents' arrival with a new leading man was accompanied by lots of whispering and speculation as seems usual in theatre companies. The new actor turned out to be a well-spoken middle sized Englishman with a big nose. His name was Hilton Edwards, and he'd had training and experience at the Old Vic. He was polite and addressed my father as 'Sir' or 'Mr. McMaster.' Micheál wrote in *All for Hecuba* that 'Mac felt fortunate to get him, but that he was bloody expensive.' Realistically, Hilton was probably glad to accept whatever salary he was offered, for it's unlikely that he would have left London so quickly if he'd had prospects of work at the time.

In spite of his youth Hilton had a bit of the 'old actor laddie' about him. He was disciplined, dressed conservatively, and expected rehearsals to begin and end on time. Poor Hilton, it must have been a shock to find he had to learn the lines of at least four important parts in about seven days, and with not enough rehearsal. Mac worked hard with Hilton and especially in the part of Iago because so many scenes in *Othello* are between the two of them and as the actor Barry Foster said; (in the tribute to Mac produced on BBC's Third Programmme soon after he died,) 'He (Mac) was very anxious that his Iago should be strong and attractive and matching his brilliance. There was no question in his mind of anyone taking a play from him.'

Very soon, Micheál and Hilton became best friends and after several months of touring they began thinking about a theatre company of their own. Hilton had all kinds of ideas for a 'new' kind of theatre of shadows and sound and abstract scenery. The direction would be stylized too and the make-up almost grotesque! Hilton's ideas were influenced by the Moscow Arts Theatre and probably too, by the Berlin theatre of the 1920s. In any case he was rarin' to go and after a year or so with Mac he and Micheál left to form their own experimental theatre in Dublin. They called it the Dublin Gate Theatre and in its original forty years existence became well known around the world.

I didn't like Hilton as an actor. He was as he was in person, too bombastic, unsubtle, full of 'sound and fury', but he was a very good director as anyone who knew the Gate in its heyday would agree. Mac was more reserved, he said that Hilton was marvellous for the overall shape of a play, crowd scenes, etc., but not so good with the individual actor. Mac didn't especially thrive under his direction, he felt it was restrictive, no room for the actor to use his own ideas, but there is no doubt that Hilton had some wonderful results. His stylized productions of *Peer Gynt* and *Mourning Becomes Electra* in the beginning were extraordinary, I believe, especially in Dublin at that time and later his more realistic productions were beautiful in their attention to detail and style. He was thoroughly organized, mapping out a production for weeks before rehearsals began, leaving nothing to chance. Rehearsals with Hilton were often painful; he could be scathing and intimidating with his actors (especially to timid ones like me). He bullied everyone, and most of all Micheál, who liked the role of martyr, put him in a good light and Hilton in a bad one. Nowadays, I can see that Hilton was in a very difficult position. Micheál was the 'star attraction,' the multi-talented and far better looking one of the two. Micheál was quick-witted and funny, Hilton was plodding and pedantic. His talents as a director and as an actor were acknowledged and greatly admired, but in his personal life he must have felt overshadowed and he retaliated with a mixture of bravado and self-pity that was not attractive.

I've often wondered what Micheál saw in Hilton, as his life's companion. Professionally, they complemented one another, each having characteristics that the other may have had but didn't necessarily want to use. For instance, Micheál had every bit as good a business sense as Hilton but, in case it made him seem unpleasant, he let Hilton do any dirty work that had to be done. On the surface they seemed an unlikely pair, but in the way my father and mother needed one another, so did Micheál and Hilton. And there was that unexplainable thing, the natural pairing of two people who for reasons unknown, are attracted to each other. With Micheál and Hilton leaving my father's company to start their own it might be imagined that rivalry would spring up between the two companies, but this wasn't so. For one thing, Micheál and Hilton established themselves solidly in Dublin, and Mac was content in the country. They did avant-garde plays that Mac found 'very interesting dear, but you can't take seriously.' In spite of their different views of the theatre, Mac would always be a 'kind of oracle' to Micheál and Hilton. The writer Christopher FitzSimon wrote in *The Boys*, his biography of the two of them, 'Anew McMaster was the only person (whose opinion) Micheál Mac Liammóir and Hilton Edwards accepted on professional matters throughout their careers although he was only a few years older.'

The year 'the boys' spent with my father was one of the most valuable periods of their lives; it prepared them for any crisis and situation that would occur in their own company. It was a crash course in all things concerning the running of a theatre company.

Touring in those days, even with a fairly large company and a stage staff, was a challenge to everyone's talent and stamina. Some faint of heart actors would, I'm sure, have fallen by the wayside if it hadn't been for Mac and his gaiety, his silly sense of fun, his stories, and imitations of the great ones of the past but most of all it was 'the performances', wrote Maurice Good, an actor in the company in the early 1950s, 'with all the stops out, when he dazzled the cast and stunned the audience into a spellbound silence before the roars of applause.'

9 – Shakespeare at the Abbey

Micheál and Hilton were now in Dublin where they first established their company at the tiny Peacock Theatre, an experimental attachment of the Abbey. Christopher and I were safely at the Norland Nurseries, so Mana didn't have to worry about us. The tours were going very well and life was falling into a routine that for the theatre was becoming reasonably settled, and perhaps for that reason it was decided to do a short tour in England. Security is not a priority with most actors, indeed it's the changeability I think that partly attracts them to the theatre. Never quite knowing what lies ahead, changes in locale, the ever-changing repertoire, the expectation of something new and exciting happening. Some actors, and my father was one, fear the tedium of a long run and the security of a weekly paycheck isn't enough as Mac found in *Paddy the Next Best Thing* when he finally broke his contract and got out of it.

To break the pattern, if nothing else, Mac agreed to the English tour. He didn't particularly like English provincial audiences who he said were unresponsive and he needed reaction from the audience, 'Otherwise' as he said, 'You're playing to a brick wall.' 'Besides' English provincial audiences are the last people in the world to appreciate Shakespeare.'

In England the company visited the ancient cities of Canterbury and Winchester, both associated with Shakespeare and Tunbridge Wells. They did reasonably well, in spite of Micheál's caustic remark, 'You can't expect faces like that' referring to the proper looking ladies in tweeds and lisle stockings 'to be interested in Shakespeare.' This English tour would not be the last however; the company would do several more over the years. Perhaps the reason for doing them was that Ireland was exhaustible for a company that toured most of the year and it wasn't good for business to return too often to the same towns.

Like everything in Mac's life the decision to do a season in Dublin's Abbey Theatre was made on the spur of the moment and by chance. He and Mana were in Dublin for a few days, he to buy more lighting which he couldn't resist, and Mana was there to see that his 'squandermania' didn't get out of hand, and one afternoon walking past the Abbey Theatre they saw that the Abbey players were on tour. At once, Mac decided that if the theatre was rentable, he would bring the company in to do a two week season beginning in December, and after a short talk with the manager, everything was settled that afternoon. The National Theatre of Ireland was barely subsidized by the government at the time and though its policy was generally to do only plays by Irish authors, the management was quite delighted, I'm sure, to bring in a little extra revenue by renting the theatre to my father.

Dublin of course had seen Shakespeare with English companies. Sir John Martin Harvey, the famous English actor-manager had visited regularly with his company, but they would do one production for a week and move on. Mac would be doing seven plays in repertory and there was the attraction too of the company being home grown, even though most of the actors were English.

Walter Humphries, the business manager and actor, was skeptical about the season being so close to Christmas. 'Theatrical suicide, total genocide,' he said, but Mac wasn't worried, his instincts told him all would be well and like an excited child he left Dublin at once to tell the company who were of course elated.

Good to be playing in the capital city and in its most distinguished theatre, and the company no doubt had visions of expansion and comfort. But the old Abbey was far from comfortable, I remember going there in my teens to see *Professor Tim* and I had to sit sideways so as not to 'bark' my knees on the seat in front. It was quite small, especially the stage which was only twenty-one feet across and about sixteen feet in depth. Amazing to think of all the great plays done there and the extraordinary actors who performed there and made this little space world famous. Actually, the McMaster Company must have felt quite at home at the Abbey. It was not unlike many of the halls they played in the country.

After winding up the tour the company converged on Dublin to rehearse. The plays would be *Hamlet, The Merchant of Venice, Othello, Macbeth, Midsummer Night's Dream, The Taming of the Shrew*, and *Romeo and Juliet*. All the plays except *Romeo* were in the repertoire on tour, so it wasn't quite as formidable as it sounds. Another advantage was that the company had been working together for nearly three years now giving them the benefit of ensemble playing which always shows in subtle ways, and so the McMaster Company, which included Micheál, Hilton, and Coralie, opened with *Hamlet*, at the Abbey in December 1927 to a packed house. Claudius was played by Hilton, who seemed to have been born to play middle aged characters even though he was several years younger than his nephew Hamlet. Micheál was a sympathetic and charming Laertes, Esme Biddle an imperious Gertrude who had the classic presence of an ancient Grecian statue, and had perfect English diction; even if she didn't always articulate correctly owing to the drink problem. Coralie Carmichael was Ophelia and somewhat miscast I'd say. She was more like Medusa in appearance than the innocent Ophelia, and J.C. Warren, the forerunner of Eugene Wellesley, was praised by *The Irish Times* for being '... the best Polonius Dublin has seen in four generations.' I don't recall who the Horatio was but it was probably David Gill. As the critic of *The Irish Independent* remarked '... unlike some actor-managers he (Mac) does not consider the best is turning the tragedy into a one man show.' Mac always wanted, but didn't always have, a strong cast around him; he wanted to be able 'to play off' the other actors and when they were really good it released the best in him.

The critic of the *Irish Statesman* was fulsome in his praise of Mac's Hamlet in a choice of words that seems strangely out of date now:

> It is not that Mr. McMaster is a great Hamlet. He is neither as noble as Forbes Robertson, nor as moving as Martin Harvey, but he is both noble and moving. He is a well-equipped and serious actor who consistently fills the stage with a graceful presence and fills his lines with music and meaning. His voice is singularly pleasing and of wide compass.

The cutting of the five hour long play was praised. 'During the first part of the play, Hamlet dominated ... but as it went on the cutting judiciously brought out the plot in a most understandable way.' So wrote Joseph Holloway, the well-known Dublin architect, who spent a lifetime going to the theatre in Dublin and wrote down all he saw in a mountain of manuscripts, now in the National Library of Ireland.

Mac's cutting of Shakespeare naturally reflected his own taste, with the emphasis on the plot, dramatic situations and the glory of the words. He wanted to leave out 'the dull bits' as much as he could in order to keep the pace moving and to try to hold the interest of the audience a hundred percent of the time. It wasn't an intellectual approach but a theatrical one. The same might be said of his acting of the part.

To my mind Hamlet was always one of Mac's great parts and certainly he had great success with it almost until the end of his life. But not everyone agreed. Harold Pinter wrote in his essay *Mac* which he dedicated to his memory that '... he was never a good Hamlet' and Mac himself didn't think he was particularly suited for the part. He felt he was too big, too robust, and that Hamlet was a tenor and he was a baritone. But except when he lashes out at Claudius and his mother and again to Laertes at Ophelia's grave, he played the part in a quiet low-key way, more introspective than was usual for him. Harold though, being an intellectual, perhaps recognized that Mac was guilty of not exploring Hamlet's inner turmoil enough. His approach was external rather than internal but for most of us that was enough.

Othello opened two days later, again to a packed house. Hilton was Iago and Micheál was Cassio. Mac was criticized for his habit of gabbling his way through the long speeches to get to the key line at the end or something that was more emotional. How strange that George Henry Lewis in his book, *On Actors and the Art of Acting*, who considered Edmond Kean to be the greatest actor of his time, should write of his Othello: 'It was, one must confess, a patchy performance considered as a whole ... some parts gabbled over in order to reach the 'points' but it was irradiated with such flashes that I would risk broken ribs for a good place in the pit to see it again.' Could Mac have been the reincarnation of this great actor? Joseph Holloway wrote of Mac's performance:

> McMaster started his Othello rather unconvincingly in his speech to the Senate. It was not until the great scenes between

him and Iago that he grew into the part and showed the very fine player he is.

The third play was *The Merchant of Venice*, which Mac almost considered a night off. He was a marvellous Shylock, proud, steely, noble, a character out of the Old Testament, orthodox and bound by traditions who, in spite of his demands, was a sympathetic character – or perhaps pathetic would be a better way to describe him. When he is broken and stripped of everything towards the end it was profoundly sad and I always thought the Christian faction had resorted to unfair tricks to disgrace him. Mac had no worries about Shylock, it fitted him like a comfortable pair of old shoes and he enjoyed it.

The basic sets that were devised out of necessity for the country and elaborated on a little for the Abbey were spoken of in *The Irish Independent*: 'The Venetian atmosphere was admirably suggested with an economy of means that other Shakespearean producers might well study.' And Joseph Holloway wrote: 'The play was beautifully dressed and lighted and set, a most artistic eye is over all.'

Macbeth was next and again the Abbey was packed. Dublin was lapping up this influx of Shakespeare. My father had all the ingredients for a magnificent Macbeth and in my view he was, but again Harold Pinter wrote: ' ... for some reason or other he rarely bothered to play Macbeth ... I believe his dislike for the play was so intense he couldn't bring himself to play it.' I disagree entirely. For me his Macbeth was on a level with his Othello, Hamlet, and King Lear, the parts he was most famous for. It's true he disliked the play but it worked in his favour, he didn't try to make the part likeable, pitiable sometimes, for here was this huge barbaric warrior who on one hand 'hates the slime that sticks on filthy deeds' but is powerless in the hands of his scheming wife. He brought out all the conflicting elements in Macbeth's nature in a savage almost ugly way and I'll always remember his agonized cries, unearthly and eerie. He was ingratiating to his guests in an oily hypocritical sort of way, cruel and plotting with Lady Macbeth and guilt ridden when he was by himself. What actor would not revel in such a part? And Mac played it with such bravado and a wicked glint in his eye that I can't think he didn't enjoy it.

I don't want it to seem that simply because I was his daughter I thought every theatrical contribution Mac made was marvellous! Not so. I've been speaking especially about the Shakespearean roles he was celebrated for and adding Oedipus to the list, but the very qualities that made Mac so right and extraordinary as a classical actor were not so easily adaptable to the modern theatre – for him anyway. He was out of place in modern plays, he was too big, and it seemed odd for him to be smoking on stage and wearing a suit and tie. He wasn't comfortable going beyond the era of the 1920s when the theatre was primarily to entertain, where there was movement and colour and dramatic situations, before the intellectual 'wordy' plays came along. 'All those words,' he'd say, 'nothing ever happens!' He made no pretense at trying to understand or like them, and just as Henry Irving or Edwin Booth would have been out of their métier in them, so was Mac.

To get back to the second week at the Abbey, three plays were done, *Romeo and Juliet*, *The Taming of the Shrew*, and *Midsummer Night's Dream*. It was an incredible undertaking, seven Shakespearean plays in twelve days. My mother must have literally not slept a wink. Her hand was in everything from coordinating the costumes and scenery, etc., to the business end of things and dealing with sometimes temperamental actors. But at least she didn't have to play seven leading parts as Mac did, familiar though he was with all of them except Oberon, of which Joseph Holloway wrote: 'McMaster's Oberon made one think he was going in for a beauty contest, he looked so imposing and handsome.' *Romeo and Juliet* was a big success and *The Irish Times*'s critic reported standing room only and said '... in the concluding scene he (Mac) gave a performance that for the beauty of its sadness has not been bettered by any Romeo.' *The Irish Independent*'s critic however had the impression ' ... that he was at least as much in love with the lovely lines as he was with Juliet!'

All in all, the Abbey Theatre season had been a triumph and Joseph Holloway wrote in summing up:

> The young actor, Anew McMaster, has proved himself a chip off the old block of great tragedians, and has made more than good as Othello, Hamlet and Romeo – in fact his Othello is a really remarkable achievement. Critic W. J. Lawrence and I are of the opinion that he will bloom into the big tragic actor of his time. He has all the natural gifts that go to make a fine actor – height, good figure, handsome clear cut face, melodious voice

of great range, and graceful gestures. He always pleases the eye as well as satisfying the mind ... If he doesn't rise to the very top, I for one will be sorely disappointed.

10 – A Second Abbey Season

Only days after the Abbey season ended, the company was on tour again, buoyed up by their success in Dublin. It had been, amongst other things, affirmation that what they were doing in the country, with all the discomforts of the touring life, was worthwhile and valuable. Mac, too, though he never really needed the approval of Dublin audiences to feel successful must have been 'well pleased' as his Aunt Dora was fond of saying, and he decided if the Abbey was available he'd do it again the following year. Might even make it a yearly event and call it 'The Dublin Shakespeare Festival.'

The new tour had only been out a few weeks when Mac was offered a leading part in a film, *The Lost Patrol*, about a British army unit lost in the desert, and off Mac went to Tunisia leaving the company to do plays he was generally not in, but he made sure that *The Merchant of Venice* would be done, as it was usually on all the schools' curriculum, and school matinees were a valuable source of income. The company continued to do *Hamlet* too without him. Mac liked to say 'the part was foolproof,' that if 'an actor has a good presence and speaks well he can't fail as Hamlet.'

Mac's experience with *The Lost Patrol* was not a happy one. There was very little water and the actors became ill with dysentery. There were difficulties of every kind and Mac was weeks late in returning home. Fortunately, he had an agreement (my mother's business sense I'm sure) that would pay him for any losses to his own company caused by delays, so home Mac eventually came, with a good deal more money in his pockets than he'd bargained for. Of course he went on a buying spree and as usual bought ever more lighting devices like the one (the very latest invention) that threw great flashes of lightning on the panorama. Mana disapproved. Supposing business was not good suddenly, they would need money to keep things going, but she kept her thoughts to herself and indulged him. As long as Mac was happy that's all that mattered.

It was about this time too that Mac bought the panatrope known as the 'pandemonium,' which was basically an electric gramophone (how archaic that sounds now) with loudspeakers. He liked to use 'incidental' music in all Shakespeare plays. He believed – as I did too since I grew up with it and missed it when other people didn't use it in their productions – that it set the tone of a scene, and created the right kind of atmosphere for things to come.

For example, 'Night on a Bare Mountain' introduced the witches in *Macbeth*, and as Desdemona I loved coming on to the gorgeous music of the 'Meditation' from *Thaïs*, and it seemed so right that the 'Liebestod' from *Tristan and Isolde* should be playing quietly in the background towards the end of the last scene of *Othello*. Naturally, Mac's great love of opera influenced him and he was of a past era when music was used freely in every play, but he was criticized for it by the Dublin critics.

As for *The Lost Patrol* it was lost indeed! One of the last silent films, it was remade into a talkie only a few years later which was a big success and the first one sank into oblivion. Mac made a few more films but it was never his cup of tea. 'All that waiting about, 'he'd say, 'The boredom would make you want to cut your throat.' More importantly film acting was not his medium. The restriction of movement, the endless re-shooting of scenes and all the technicalities took away the very thing that illuminated his performances, his moments of inspiration and spontaneity. Besides, he needed an audience!

Back on tour, Mac was doing more melodrama, why not, they all had marvellous, leading roles; flamboyant and macabre, sinister and often outrageously funny. Most actors would love to do them sometime in their careers I'm sure, and the Irish country audiences accepted them eagerly. After all, Mac became an actor-manager to do exactly as he wanted!

When the second festival at the Abbey was arranged, Mac decided as well as Shakespeare, to do *Richard III, The School for Scandal,* and three melodramas, *David Garrick,* about the 18th century actor, and like *The Scarlet Pimpernel*, good entertainment but hardly a work of art, and *Mr. Wu*, about a mysterious man from China.

Mac invited a much-loved figure in the theatre to join him for the next Abbey season. He was Sir Frank Benson, and to a young actor nowadays it must be like talking of Sarah Siddons or at least Henry Irving. In fact, Benson was just beginning his career as Henry Irving was in the midst of doing his endless string of farewell tours. Benson was 70 or thereabouts and going towards the end of his own long career as an actor-manager when Mac asked him to come to Dublin to play Sir Peter Teazle in *The School for Scandal* and Shylock in *The Merchant* which he was pleased to do, since it was difficult for actors to retire, something that hasn't changed much. In spite of powerful trade unions, most actors have to keep working or live in poverty – even knighted ones!

The second Abbey season opened in December 1928, exactly a year after the first. The company was large and strong but missing were Micheál, Hilton and Coralie who had moved to the Gate Theatre, their new home, and were now completely involved in their own productions.

The company opened again with *Hamlet* and the reviews were even better than the year before, praising Mac and the company and the 'simple, yet decorative settings enabling him (Mac) to speed up the action...' so wrote Joseph Holloway, but he also said, 'It's curious that he should hamper himself with musical accompaniment in certain scenes. Not only is the orchestra irrelevant, it's strains however delicately modulated, clash incongruously with the rhythm of Shakespeare's verse.'

On 6 December, *The School for Scandal* opened and Joseph Holloway wrote, 'A great house of playgoers filled the Abbey to welcome back Sir Frank Benson, who had not played in Dublin for 25 years.' He went on to say that he played with 'great spirit and much energy,' and that 'It was a night of rare enthusiasm and the old actor must have been thrilled by his reception after so many years.'

Mr. Wu was the third play that season and it too played to packed houses. I remember the play only vaguely as it disappeared from the repertoire when I was about twelve or thirteen and none too soon apparently. It was one of the 'frightful plays' as Micheál called them in *All for Hecuba*, 'but,' he continued, 'there are certain parts in poor plays that give an actor an astounding freedom of interpretation, ... moulding them to his or her will as the greatest parts with their inexorable structure refuse to be moulded.' I'm not sure that this is true. In the end, you go to another performance of *Hamlet*, not just to see *Hamlet* again, but another actor's interpretation. Mac knew of course that *Mr. Wu* was balderdash, but it had a tremendous part for him, his excuse for doing several of the plays he did.

The ever present Mr. Holloway wrote:

> There was a great house for *Mr. Wu* ... from the moment Mr. Wu entered, the play caught fire and held the entire audience to the end of the play. In fact, the tension during the last scene was almost painfully intense and Anew McMaster's Mr. Wu dominated the scene.'

Next was *The Merchant of Venice* with Frank Benson as Shylock. Mr. Holloway called it a 'truly memorable performance.' But *The Irish Times* critic spoke of the difference between 'the naturalistic style of the company and such a performance as Frank Benson gives us'.

I have a good idea of the style of Frank Benson's acting, having known Eugene Wellesley as long as I did. Eugene was the leading character actor in our company for many years and a dear friend. He had spent his early years with Sir John Martin Harvey, the much honoured actor-manager in England. Martin Harvey was to Eugene what Fred Terry had been to Mac. Eugene's love for 'his dearly departed little master' as he called him made him want to be as like him as possible, and as Frank Benson was of the same period with the same traditions and influences it's not difficult to imagine his style.

It was the time of 'exterior' acting when you never turned your back on the audience, you made sure you died on stage in a graceful position, and you showed the best side of your face as much as possible, you never upstaged another actor, (unless you're an egotist) and there were the little tricks, like clapping your hands when another actor slaps you on the face. These things I remember so well from Eugene, but naturally too there was still that particular talent that made these actors special in their time and I don't wish to disparage Benson or Harvey. It was simply a different era. Sarah Bernhardt was a great actress but with the changes now in style and technique, would we still think so?

It may have crossed the reader's mind that surely my father, with his heart and mind in a past era, may have had leanings towards acting in the way I've described. Yes, of course he did, that's why he did melodramas like *Mr. Wu, David Garrick,* and *The Bells* to indulge himself and to live, at least, for a couple of hours in that time, but his performances in them had nothing to do with his acting of Shakespeare or anything else.

Mac played only one performance of *Richard III* at the Abbey that season, probably because he wasn't sure enough of the words! He'd had no breaking in period on tour, and when he was unsure it always showed. It couldn't have been a complete disaster though. *The Irish Independent* critic wrote: '[Richard] was no mere canting rogue, neither is he the suave, cold villain of the type Machiavelli is supposed to have created. He is very human with moments of splendour in his sins.'

David Garrick was the last play that season, a melodrama that Mac couldn't resist. *The Irish Times* wrote all that needs to be said and affirms the above:

> Mr. McMaster departed from his usual intimate and reserved style for the occasion and transported his audience back to the good old-fashioned style. The piece was played for pure comedy in the most unrestrained manner.

11 – Enter Mrs Patrick Campbell and Williamstown

As was becoming routine, the company went straight back on tour after closing at the Abbey. My brother Christopher and I, at three-and-a half and two-and-a half years, respectively, had outgrown the Norland Nurseries and had begun our own odyssey of staying with 'aunties' and 'uncles'. According to some faded snaps I still have – and the only way I have of knowing where we were about this time – we stayed first with 'Aunt' Emily Perrin, Mana's old friend at her lovely ivy covered manor house in Bushy Heath outside London. Then Mac and Mana brought us for the first time on tour with them in the southwest of Ireland, but it must have been difficult for my mother and us for soon afterwards we were sent to stay with Peter McCormack in an enormous dilapidated 18th-century mansion in County Meath. Peter, despite her name was actually a woman; although by the way she dressed and strode about the estate it might have been difficult to tell. She was 'county' as we called it, or more correctly, she belonged to the Ascendancy class, which was then in Ireland fast coming to mean that she was well bred, Protestant, and impoverished.

Williamstown, as the estate was called, was huge and desolate. Room after room, high-ceilinged, with beautiful Italian marble fireplaces and intricately designed plasterwork, were all empty. Peter and an elderly retainer and Chris and I all lived in three fairly comfortable rooms downstairs next to the vast kitchen, also not used because Peter's hens and pigs lived there!

Williamstown became very much part of our childhood. We'd stay there off and on until I was about six and after that in holidays from boarding school. I loved it, we were like little animals Chris and I, free as the wind to come and go, to wear clothes or not if we didn't want to. We swam in the river with Rollie and Moses, Peter's two collies who I adored, and we rode on the tractor and 'helped' with the seeding and ploughing. I'm not sure who was in charge of us, certainly Peter wasn't.

It was during our first visit to Williamstown that Mac and Mana made arrangements for what turned out to be the last season at the Abbey. It would be for just one week as the theatre had been previously rented to the 'Civil Service Dramatic Society,' a double rejection for Mac, who without knowing anything about them decided all government employees were dreary and dull; and he never liked the idea of people whose life's work it wasn't 'getting up on stage and think they can act.'

Mac, wanting to make the short week at the Abbey as exciting as possible, invited Mrs Patrick Campbell, England's great tragic actress, to come to Dublin to play Lady Macbeth with him, and Mrs Alving in *Ghosts* and to his surprise she agreed, writing dramatically that she'd always wanted to 'tread the boards of Yeats, Synge and Lady Gregory'.

Mrs Campbell, in her early 60s at this time, was still reigning queen of the English theatre and next to his undying adoration for Madame Sarah; in Mac's eyes she could do no wrong. He wasn't at all put off by her reputation for being difficult to work with and said he'd put up with anything just to play opposite her – and he did. Mac described the last season at the Abbey as 'The most exhilarating, exciting if not the most peaceful theatrical experience of my life.'

Mrs Campbell seemed to be sweetness itself in the preliminary letters and telegrams that went back and forth between Mac and her. She agreed to the terms Mac suggested, said that a suite at the Shelbourne would do nicely, and because she was coming to Ireland she'd had all her luggage painted bright green.

She arrived by the mail boat with great fanfare. Mac assumed the role of some head of state greeting visiting royalty, and escorted her to the Shelbourne, Dublin's conservative and most beautiful hotel. This was where she decided most of the rehearsals should take place.

My mother had known 'Mrs Pat' years before through her friendship with her daughter, Stella, when both had been art students at the Slade School and they shared a flat together for a time. Mrs Pat would breeze in once in a while smothered in furs and Pekinese dogs and tell Stella in the hoarse throaty voice she was famous for, that it was not possible for human life to survive in such sordid conditions. Mana was actually delighted with their tiny but well-ordered flat and, for Stella, I imagine it was freedom from tyranny, for Mrs Pat, who was charming and exciting and dramatic could also be 'a bloody bitch' as Mana remembered.

At any event it was probably Mana's acquaintance with Mrs Pat that opened the doors for her to come to Dublin. It's doubtful she would have known who Mac was otherwise. He'd been out of the public eye in London for several years and was most often 'lost in the bogs of Ireland' as Ivor Novello had said.

'Rehearsals began fairly smoothly,' Mana wrote for Mac in *The Irish Times* articles, 'except that, first she'd be too hot, so that we had to open all the windows, then she'd be too cold so we promptly had to close them again, but these small things didn't matter because she was so exciting to work with ... 'But as the days went by, Mrs Pat began to show her difficult side and Mac continued, at least for the present, to insist that if one has to put up with certain problems, it was worth it because she was such a great artist.

From *All for Hecuba*, Micheál wrote an account of the rehearsals as they progressed: '... as the days went by Mac began to agree with the jealous ones who had complained of her caprices. 'She's pure heaven!' he repeated on the first Monday and Tuesday, 'and not a word of that stuff about her being difficult is true.' On Wednesday he came to tea looking a little worn. 'Of course she's such a great actress you see,' he began, 'you have to forgive a great actress if she ... well, you have to overlook these little moments, that's all.' On Thursday he said, 'I suppose she is as great as ... yes she is. She is! But there are things in her character that ... no, I won't say it.' Friday arrived – 'Oh the things she said today!' he said, flinging himself on the sofa, 'The moods, the sulks, the venom. Oh well, let's forget it, that's all we can do.' But in the middle of the following week, no doubts were left.

'Today, dear, I saw, with my own eyes what people mean about her,' he cried, striding up and down the room and breathing through his nose.

> Don't mention her to me, don't breathe her bloody name. She's a fiend, dear, ... in human shape! God, I didn't think it possible that any human being could be such a ----- Oh well, never again

that's all I can say. My God, never again! It's no use and I shall always adore the wicked bitch. You see, in spite of everything she's such an incredible artist.

And his worship, whole hearted, ungrudging and badly mauled, lasted 'til the end'. Naturally in the telling of this, Micheál embellished and exaggerated a bit. He couldn't help it, he was an actor, he liked to entertain, and that he did – no question.

Stories about Mrs Pat and her shenanigans were rampant in Dublin at the time. She seemed to have a knack of finding out the weakness in people and then embarrass them by 'exposing' them in front of others. One of Mac's friends decided she was possessed and should be exorcized!

Rehearsals were marked by tantrums and undermining remarks to the younger players. She insisted that the opening of *Ghosts* be postponed because she needed an extra day of rehearsal, but the manager of the Abbey persuaded her to open as scheduled. She did, and the result was not a happy one. She was uncertain of her lines and seemed very nervous. At the curtain call she thanked the audience 'for their generous applause' which she said was scarcely deserved because 'we have not done justice to this great tragedy,' and she pointed out the 'unevenness and scrappiness, which marked this performance.'

She had asked for one more day of rehearsal but would it have made any great difference? I suppose it would because when the play was done again two days later, she and the cast were all certain of their lines and 'even Mrs Pat played with ease, ' as Mr. Holloway wrote, and in spite of all, the play received excellent reviews.

In *All for Hecuba*, Micheál wrote about her performance as Mrs Alving:

> Her performance was an astounding affair, and had about as much to do with Ibsen's play as the Aubrey Beardsley illustrations have to do with Wilde's Salome. No mother of a stricken man, no homely provincial Norwegian could have looked and spoken as she did and yet she moved about the stage sighing, laughing, and weeping, her smallest gesture a graven image of significance and beauty, that monstrous magnetism of hers held fast and Hilton muttered thickly in my ear, 'She's forgotten more than any of us will ever know.'

It had all been worth it, as Mac knew it would be.

Mrs Pat played with him in *Macbeth* too and one night when I was at the side of the stage during the performance, she sailed up to me with a banana in her hand. 'I've bought that out of my own money for your poor thin little sister', she proclaimed in that curious whisper of hers like soft thunder among dry reeds. 'You will give it to her won't you, nice, kind boy? I'm sure Mac starves her.'

Another version of the banana story, as Mana wrote for Mac in *The Irish Times* articles:

> She swooped down on Marjorie curled up in a corner of a sofa. She had a banana in one hand and a bottle of port in the other and transfixing my wife with great blazing eyes, she thrust her offering into her lap muttering: 'Poor little thing, I believe that great hulk of a husband starves you. Eat this and drink some port, it will bring some colour into those poor pale cheeks.'

As for Mrs Pat's Lady Macbeth, it was enthusiastically applauded but Mr. Holloway wrote rather ungallantly that '... she had fallen into flesh and much of the beauty of her voice had vanished into a sort of hoarse whisper.' But that she was 'most effective in the sleepwalking scene ... '

The iconic Mrs Patrick Campbell (Mr Campbell incidentally was said to have gone off to the Boer War to get himself killed because he couldn't put up with Mrs Campbell another second) is long a part of theatre history now. The realization that I was there and so was Christopher serves to remind me of my own advancing years and how exciting it would have been if we had been old enough to remember. Chris was almost four and I was nearly three when Mrs Pat brought us both on stage at the Abbey after a matinee of *Macbeth*. Christopher, always calm and obedient – outwardly at least – allowed himself to be taken by the hand and stood looking wondrously out at the audience, while I, incensed and outraged, was carried on pounding and beating Mrs Pat's face in a frantic effort to get away. This was probably the beginning of my life-long struggle with stage fright. As for Mrs Pat, in the midst of all the commotion she kept smiling and bowing. It brought down the house, as she knew it would.

12 – Hard Times

With the success of the three seasons at the Abbey, Mac began thinking of having his own permanent theatre in Dublin. Somewhere large enough to attract general audiences at reasonable prices and he found the Tivoli, an old variety house closed for several years and he, Walter, and my mother made a bid for it, but it wasn't meant to be, as Éamon de Valera suddenly bought it and turned it into a printing works for his newspaper, *The Irish Press*. Mac was terribly disappointed and went to bed for several days with a stocking tied around his eyes. But I'm sure he hadn't considered the difficulties of running a permanent establishment, a business, and without government subsidies and grants. Even Micheál and Hilton with their small Gate Theatre found the going rough at times.

Ireland's country towns were to be Mac's destiny. Moreover, touring suited his restlessness, allowing him to do as he pleased, to indulge himself in some 'frightful' plays as Micheál called them. They often also allowed him sometimes to be 'naughty' by taking liberties with them; something that would not have gone unnoticed by the city critics. An argument might be that if he were playing to the critics and to more sophisticated audiences, he'd have had to be more disciplined, which ultimately would have been a good thing but, as I pointed out, to control Mac would have been to inhibit him. It was the freedom he had with his own company in the country that allowed him to reach the extraordinary heights, later so memorably described by Harold Pinter, that he was capable of.

The next couple of years followed the usual pattern. The Shakespeare always remained, but other plays, good and bad came and went, and actors did too. At the end of a tour, they would go back to their homes then usually in England. Mac and Mana too would go back to their flat in London, which they still kept, in spite of their lives now being permanently in Ireland. Mac never quite lost the persona of a London actor; it was where he began, where he had his first training and experience. He understood the life, the camaraderie, the jargon, and his early theatre friends were still there. Did he have hopes of acting there again one day, in spite of his vow never to do so? Of course he did, and certainly if something worthwhile fell into his lap (as it did occasionally) he'd have leaped at it. On the other hand, another good reason for touring Ireland was that he loathed having to look for work. It was humiliating to him, like having to ask someone for a loan. Besides he was too grand. He had this air of extravagance and opulence about him. He was not competitive and his psyche was too fragile to deal with rejection, especially when things weren't going well and were beginning to change as they dramatically did when the 1929 stock market crash in the United States had its effect on the whole world as a poor, newly independent Ireland, trying desperately to recover from centuries of domination by the British, fell further into poverty and unemployment.

The theatre was naturally one of the first casualties. The people were having trouble eating and certainly there was no money for entertainment. Mac kept the price of admission ridiculously low and the company managed to keep going but still all was far from well. By the beginning of the 1930s, talking pictures and all the fascination of something new had begun to invade the country towns, at least the ones who could afford the new audio equipment, and the company which had generally played to full houses were now playing to a handful. Eventually the novelty wore off and the live theatre and the films managed to continue in peaceful coexistence, but not before it had taken a toll.

Mac and Mana decided to disband the company and my father had no alternative but to head off to England to look for work. He made the rounds and after nothing turned up he 'lowered' himself as he liked to say by taking a job in weekly repertory, in Leicester, a deadly move for him. The depressing atmosphere of a Northern English industrial city in the middle of an economic slump, doing a different play every week, and Mac's difficulty with learning lines and most of all being without Mana, was a lethal combination. He called it 'hell on earth!' It was one of the few times in his life that he was forced to do something he didn't want to do.

My mother wrote sadly about seeing him off at the station and returning alone to 'a dark little room' (the flat had been sublet) 'and so there we are, Mac speeding off to Leicester ... and Chris and Mary-Rose far off in the spacious peace of Williamstown and here am I alone in a tiny stuffy little room, silent as the grave...'

Would we not have been a comfort to her? Perhaps she felt we were better off at Williamstown and we were, but that was to change too. The time had come for us to go to school. It would seem natural since Chris and I were at Williamstown so much of the time for us to go to school in Ireland, but because Mana's older sister, Dorothy Old, known as Doff, ran a small boarding school in the south of England, she decided I should go there and, for a short time, Chris went there too.

It was a huge upheaval; I didn't want to go to England. Ireland was where I belonged and apparently I let everyone around me know this, because I turned into a frightened hysterical wild animal! Poor Mana, I literally had to be pried off her, as she handed me over to Aunt Doff.

I was (I've been told) very uncooperative the first few days at Lancing, hiding in a cupboard under the stairs and screaming at anyone who came near me. Chris fitted in quietly and submissively; whatever he was feeling, he kept inside, but he often looked sad and his eyes became bigger and rounder.

We both quickly adjusted as children do and I grew to love it at Lancing and Aunt Doff. I remember that first day. We sat at the kitchen table and ate boiled eggs. Why do I remember such an insignificant thing? Perhaps because it was so comforting and warm. I can still see the blue and white tablecloth and the brown earthenware teapot and the ordered way the table was set. I remember 'Mrs Old', as I had to call my aunt, with her low calming voice. How was I, a rampaging out of control little monster, able to absorb this peaceful little scene? I was about five and it's one of my earliest memories, I suppose like most things in my family, my shenanigans were greatly exaggerated.

Mrs Old became my rock, my security in every way, she was constant, unchanging, unaffected and she presided over her small group of pupils (about 15 day pupils and 3 or 4 boarders) with gentle discipline and kindness. I grew to love her very much and she was the only person in the family, who, perhaps because she had nothing to do with the theatre, told the truth absolutely!

As the years went by I always knew to go to her if I wanted to know the real story. How did Doc, my grandfather, really die? The story was that the exhaust from his car asphyxiated him. Did my grandmother (Mary or Sophie depending who you were talking to) really drown when she fell into a well? Neither is true. What about Aunt Christine who died in Africa after being bitten on the shoulder by a monkey? Not true. These stories were invented by Micheál who seemed to have an aversion to allowing people in the family to die natural deaths. To do justice to my little mother, who wouldn't, I believe, have made up such things, but she was always loyal to Micheál and when he told a 'whopper' as she called it, she would never have contradicted him. The billows of mystery that surrounded Micheál's origin could easily have been explained by Aunt Doff, as I later called her, but I didn't have any reason to question it and it was never discussed until both were gone.

Down the road from Viking House School (so English) lived Aunt Peg, the youngest of Mana and Micheál's sisters. She was very like Micheál to look at except for her colouring, which was fair, and she was dramatic like him too. She was married to Billy Higginbottom, an artist, well known for his book, *The Frightfulness of Modern Art*, but Aunt Peg was a widow in the days of my schooling, and so was Aunt Doff whose husband, Norman Old had died when he fell from a ladder and hit his head on a lavatory – but it may have been Micheál who told me that.

As much as I loved my years at Lancing, it was not home. Even with the insecurities of moving about all the time, Ireland was where I belonged, but despite my two English aunts, with their unmistakably English accents and names, it did not enter my head that we were more English – in blood – than Irish.

When I'd been at Lancing a few months, Daddy came to visit. Chris had already left and gone to a boys school in Essex. Daddy arrived in a pale grey beautifully tailored suit (do I remember this, or is it something Mrs Old told me?) and a soft wide-brimmed hat. He was the knight, the Prince Charming of everyone's dreams; handsome, funny, glorious. He brought presents for the other boarders as well as me and hid them all over the house and even in the trees in the garden. He was a child, enjoying it as much as us, looking fiendish and knowing one moment as he tried to get us off the scent of finding something, and screaming with glee when we did! Then suddenly he was gone, and for the next few days I felt special and very important, no one I had a father like mine.

13 – Stratford

Difficulties with learning lines plagued Mac all his life. His weekly repertory in Leicester was agony, even though he had been able to arrange for two or three plays from his own repertoire to be included and even though he knew those well, the strain of it all wore him down; besides, it was foolish of him to think he could function without my mother on or off the stage. So after just a few weeks he gave his notice and went back to London, not having a notion of what was coming next. One thing was certain, he swore, even if it meant the poor house, he would never do weekly repertory again!

Mac once more made the rounds of London, looking as if he'd just walked out of Saville Row, with his elegantly tailored suits, the handmade shoes and silk shirts. When things were not going well he looked particularly opulent, he rode about in taxis, and ate at expensive restaurants. Sometimes he had to 'pop' (pawn) his gold cigarette case or his watch, to keep this up, 'If you're down you don't want the world to know it,' he'd say. He was right of course, prospective managers are much more likely to offer you work when you're looking prosperous, than when you look as if your life depended on it!

It worked for Mac anyway and one day while he was having lunch with his old friends Ivor Novello and Bobbie Andrews, Phyliss Nielson-Terry, the daughter of his old mentor Fred Terry, walked in and announced that Oscar Asche, from Mac's Australian past, was in town to do a new production of *The Merry Wives of Windsor*. Mac went at once to see his old friend, and Oscar, having had no news of Mac since he disappeared from the London scene seven years before, was delighted to see him, and had imagined him to be dead and buried. He cast my father as Ford, and Mac was once again in the swim of the London Theatre and it was good, but not for long, for in spite of having many well-known London actors in the cast and Oscar himself had always been a draw in London, the play didn't do well and lasted only a couple of weeks. But out of the failure of *Merry Wives* came one of the highest points, though not the happiest times, in Mac's career.

One evening W. Bridges Adams, the director of the new Shakespeare Memorial Theatre in Stratford-on-Avon went to see *Merry Wives* and was impressed by Mac's performance and he wrote in his biography: 'He was not the best Ford I had ever seen, but there was a distinction about him that seemed to isolate him from the rest.'

Bridges Adams remembered seeing Mac act once before in a very different setting when he and his wife were on a fishing holiday in County Kerry. They decided – after a dreary day of catching no fish and noting a play bill advertising that Anew McMaster and his company were playing in nearby Cahirciveen, – to go to a performance of *The Cardinal*. 'The mounting of the play impressed us,' he wrote,

> ... on a stage barely wide enough to hold *The Cardinal* ... there was an effect of spaciousness, of richness, of rightness as to the period and taste that one did not always get in the West End of London. Even the lighting was imaginative proceeding from a battery of lamps that were certainly not supplied by Cahirciveen ... my first sight of McMaster was enough to reveal there he had the essential touch of royalty about him, and it sent me home with the conviction that at least there was one large fish to be caught in Ireland.

Bridges Adams invited Mac to come to Stratford to be one of the three leading men. He would be *Coriolanus*, Bolingbroke in *Richard II*, and Macduff in *Macbeth*. *Hamlet* was to be done also, but Hamlet itself had not been cast. I can imagine the unspoken competition between the actors but Mac felt sure it wouldn't be him.

At first Mac wasn't sure he wanted to do it, challenges made him nervous and he was never at his best when he felt pressured, but he agreed eventually, probably with the prodding of my mother who was always more ambitious for him than he was.

Coriolanus was a challenge, Mac had never even read it and when he did said he wasn't much impressed. It was also one of the longest plays in Shakespeare and studying it horrified him. Mac's inability to learn lines easily had a much more serious impact on his life than anyone knew at the time. It undermined his confidence and coloured his decisions to take or not take an engagement that could have been rewarding.

I wonder sometimes if my father wouldn't have had a greater sense of achievement if he'd taken on new parts more often. The price for him and for everyone around him I think would have been too great. When he began the study of a new part, which of course he did from time to time, we all knew we were in for months of hell!

His 'method' of learning lines was peculiar and painful. He'd pick out the first letters of each word in a sentence and repeat them over and over, so that for 'Go you before Gloucester with these letters' he'd learn G.Y.B.G.W.T.L. It made no sense! It almost seemed that he looked at the words on the page as if they were an unknown language and he was learning them phonetically without understanding their meaning. Eventually after months (which he had with his own company) and when he felt sure enough not to have to think of what was coming next, he was set free to play with a part, dance with it, and to bring his own special magic to it.

So it was with some apprehension that Mac went to Stratford. He felt himself to be in a weak position joining the company later than everyone else and he knew he'd have no breaking-in period.

The rehearsals lasted all day and were run on a strict schedule that reminded Mac of factory workers clocking in and clocking out. His usual sense of fun and silliness temporarily vanished. Mac with all his panache and sophistication had never quite overcome the insecurities of his childhood. The lack of affection, the isolation, the feeling that whatever he did wasn't good enough, all came to the surface and if he could have escaped, as he usually did in times of stress, he would have, but there was also his pride and perhaps leaving would have been a greater blow to it than staying.

However, when he made his mind up about liking or disliking a situation or someone, Mac seldom changed his mind, and he was quite determined to feel persecuted at Stratford. He imagined the other actors were whispering about him behind his back, especially when he was struggling with words. He vanished as soon as rehearsals ended and hid himself and us in a cottage called Loxley in the country several miles from Stratford.

Loxley was a perfect well preserved Elizabethan cottage, a doll's house, everything about it was tiny. I was young, only seven, but I can still see the heavy oak beams in the sitting room so low that Daddy had to bend double not to bang his head. I remember the little staircase lined with shiny brass warming pans that led to the tiny bedrooms, and the diamond shaped leaded glass in the windows and how Daddy could easily reach up and touch us when he was in the garden below. Loxley was like living in a fairy tale for Chris and me but for Mana it was a very difficult time, she was constantly worried about Mac and the strain he was under. The strain must have been enormous and for the whole company too. Four new productions opening in the first week! Enough to have thrown even the most hardened weekly rep. actors into a frenzy. The plays were *Much Ado About Nothing, Macbeth, As You Like It,* and *Richard II*. Mac was lucky he was only in three of them and these he was familiar with, but he was still working with new directors in new productions and looming up was *Coriolanus* to open the second week.

Macbeth was especially difficult for Mac, the traditionalist, he must have been completely 'nonplussed' by Komisarjevski's production with its 'aluminum spiral towers and mirrors and nightmare effects and the actors all dressed in Nazi uniforms with helmets and pot scourers for epaulettes' so wrote Mana in the *Times* articles. Not impressed, Mac decided to go his own way. 'He was a tremendous Macduff,' the actress Rachel Kempson said, 'but it was a solo.' Carl Falb, in his thesis wrote, '...and so it seems, because he got very good notices for being a traditional Macduff in an untraditional setting.' And he quoted the critic of the *London Daily Express,*

> The result of knocking the two chief performances end wise ... was that when Anew McMaster ... gave us a piece of straight strong acting excellently spoken, he had the chief personal success of the evening.

Next for Mac was Bolingbroke in *Richard II* and the *Daily Express* critic said Mac was '... this year's chief new acquisition.' However, the critic of the *Christian Science Monitor* remarked on Mac's little weakness and he wrote, 'Mr. McMaster's relative failure to get the full orchestral music out of Shakespeare's verse was due mainly I think, to insufficient familiarity with Bolingbroke's lines!'

As You Like It was the third play that first week and Mac played Jacques, not an especially demanding part and as it has no 'great scene', he must have felt it was hardly worth studying. For years later with his own company he was still not sure of Jacques' lines!

Even so, it had been a gruelling week and Mac had only the weekend to be ready for *Coriolanus* and even with rehearsals going fairly well he knew he was far from ready. Mana stayed up with him all night endlessly going over and over lines, humouring him, soothing him, trying to keep up his spirits.

What she did with Chris and me, I've no idea, but I'm sure we were kept out of Mac's way. Christopher though was important, for he was playing Marcus, Coriolanus' son. He was eight years old at the time, not six as Mana wrote in *The Irish Times*. The accuracy of dates and facts was never important in my family, but Chris always seemed younger than he was. Even when he was grown and had children of his own he had about him a look of innocent bewilderment, that if someone had whispered that he was temporarily visiting from another planet, and he knew nothing of the goings on of this one, you'd not have been surprised.

With his very private nature, it might have been difficult for him to exhibit himself on stage, but Chris didn't allow outside situations to interfere with his inner self and it's quite probable that he could have been drawing 'eye pictures' (drawings in his head) of the map of Europe while saying his lines as Marcus. In any case, Marcus was noted by one critic who wrote: '... his few lines were delivered in a sweet clear piping voice.'

Mac managed to rise to the occasion for the opening of *Coriolanus,* and only Mana could have detected the moments when he was unsure. Bridges Adams, who directed it, wrote in his autobiography: 'McMaster's performance is still remembered. It had a classic simplicity, seldom has that noble, but incorruptible, adolescent been presented with so little psychological fuss. He did not make points, he was, and he charged through the part and his great moments were the natural emanation of his spirit. I recall ... his tenderness with his young wife ... and of course his death, he shouted with laughter as the knives went in, died on his feet, and fell with a crash like a column in the Place Vendôme.'

Mac and the production had generally good notices but one or two critics picked out '... certain mannerisms which he (Mac) could well be rid of'. The *Morning Post* said, '... he (was the discovery of this year's festival, but that effort was evident almost all the time.' The *Daily Telegraph* remarked: 'He mouths his words too much and is inclined to grimace at moments of emotional stress.' The critic didn't know of course that the whole part caused him emotional stress! It was when he was not positive of what was coming next, when he was not 'rotten perfect' of the words as he called it, 'mouthing the words and grimacing' was his agonizing way of summoning them up. He was physically going through labour pains giving birth to the words.

I'm not sure that Mac had enough performances of *Coriolanus* ever to feel 'rotten perfect', but he grew to love the part and wanted to include it in his own repertory in Ireland, but he never did because it required huge crowd scenes which would have been difficult on some of the small stages as well as having to recruit them from the local townspeople.

In spite of his difficulties the critics and audiences generally had approved, so Mac was doing well. The company and directors were all friendly, he'd made a very good impression and there was no reason for him to feel persecuted, but it was the attitude he'd adopted and logic and argument could not change it, not even when to his huge surprise he was chosen from the three leading men to play the first Hamlet at the new theatre in Stratford.

The fact that he was to be the very first Hamlet in the new Memorial Theatre, a part no doubt coveted by the other actors, and his feelings that they envied him, only added to Mac's persecution complex. He withdrew to Loxley, rehearsing during the day and playing at night and otherwise keeping entirely to himself. Mana, trying no doubt to snap him out of it, told him he was like 'a bear with a sore bottom' and that he should count his blessings. He was of course honoured and very pleased to have been the chosen one, but there would be difficulties. Although *Hamlet* had been a fixture in his own company since the beginning, Mac was used to doing a cut version, as was the practice with most companies but Bridges Adams, who was directing and known as 'Unabridges Adams', cut nothing and Mac had to re-study it as though it was a new part, more difficult in fact since fitting in new scenes with ones already known is always tricky.

I've already spoken of my opinion of my father's Hamlet, I loved it. Yes, it was an 'outward' approach. He didn't go into the psychological ramifications of Hamlet, but could anyone top the anguish in his voice when he discovers that it is Ophelia who is being buried? 'Twenty thousand brothers and all their love could not make up my sum.' It was wild, frantic, and filled with infinite regret.

Mac's reviews were mixed. One critic picked up on his 'exterior' rather than 'interior' approach and hauled him over the coals for it. Two of them had conflicting thoughts, almost as if they'd seen two different actors playing it. One said:

> There is nothing to be said for Mr. Anew McMaster's shouting, screaming, storming Hamlet ... instead of quietly exploring his way through the maze of Hamlet's mind, he tries to crash his way through it.

The other said:

> His rendering lacked nothing in intelligence, but a good deal in emotional power. He seemed, in fact to have been so careful to give meaning to the words that he lost touch with the feelings that inspired them!

Yes, of course there have been mixed opinions about Mac's Hamlet. In Ireland, he could do no wrong, his Hamlet was lauded by the critics and his audiences over and over for years, and I don't believe that because the audiences were mostly made up of unsophisticated country people their opinion is not to be valued. The Irish are well known for their 'gift of the gab.' It is a natural attribute to appreciate poetic language, so it was with Shakespeare which they always flocked to and they could tell too, when thoughts and emotions were 'play acting' and when they were really felt. They had a genuine ear for it and Mac did not feel that this was so with their equivalent in England.

Mac used to say that there was too much analysing amongst the play-going intellectuals in England. 'It's all very well,' he might have said 'that I'm guilty of not gently exploring my way through the maze of Hamlet's mind'. A maze is a tangled frustrating puzzle. The audience doesn't want to be subjected to that, while the actor playing Hamlet, thinks, pauses, ruminates, and sighs. So bloody boring! In other words, Mac had no time for 'pregnant pauses', it wasn't theatrically effective. It works wonderfully in film, when one sees the workings of a man's mind, through the tiny imperceptible raising of an eyebrow, or the slight quivering of the mouth. The camera picks up everything, but I don't think this is so in the theatre.

Mac's Hamlet was quiet, even reserved for the most part, and it was beautiful to listen to and heart breaking; he 'thought' with his heart rather than his brain and the result was often extraordinary, mesmerizing, but no, it was not an intellectual approach and his critics picked up on it.

It had been, on balance, such a successful season for him, on that opening year of the new theatre it was a pity that Mac was so bent on not enjoying it. He'd made a very good impression in all the plays but *Hamlet*, but when he was asked by a fan if he would be back the next year, he answered, 'Not unless I'm bloody starving, dear!'

1 Anew McMaster, aged 17

2 Mac in London, aged 20

3 Mary-Rose's mother, Marjorie Willmore (Mana) taken before the First World War

4 Anew McMaster at the height of his career

5 Early photo of Anew McMaster as Othello

6 Anew McMaster as Hamlet as he appeared in the lead role at Stratford

7 Mac and Marjorie visiting Mary-Rose and Christopher at Norland Nurseries in London

8 Christopher and Mary-Rose at the Norland Nurseries (an expensive children's home run by 'drill sergeants')

9 Life-size portrait by the Italian artist, Gaetano De Gennaro, of Anew McMaster as Othello

10 Mary-Rose's brother, Christopher, as Fleance in *Macbeth*

11 Mary-Rose as a very unwilling Fleance in another production of *Macbeth*

12 Anew McMaster as Shylock in *The Merchant of Venice*

13 At home, 1947, sharing picnic with American film stars. Left to right: Paulette Goddard, Anew McMaster, Burgess Meredith, and Mana

14 Micheál MacLiammóir in his recital, 'The Importance of Being Oscar'.
Photograph by *The Times,* London

15 Early photograph of Mary-Rose

16 Anew McMaster in *King Lear*

17 At the Dublin Theatre Festival, 1961. Left to Right: Brendan Smith; Robert Briscoe, Lord Mayor of Dublin; Mary-Rose with her late husband, Jack Aranson, who played Ahab in *Moby Dick*

18 Mary-Rose's parents sharing a light moment, with their family dog Olga, at the front of 57 Strand Road, Sandymount, facing Dublin Bay, 1962, the year of Anew McMaster's death. The house was previously owned by the writer Frank O'Connor

THE IRISH TIMES

13 D'OLIER STREET, DUBLIN 2
THURSDAY, JANUARY 4, 1996

Appreciation

Christopher McMaster

Christopher McMaster, who died recently at his home in Hampshire at the age of 70, was a distinguished television director, although his earlier career was spent as an actor in Ireland, Britain and Australia. He was born in London in 1925, the first child and only son of the actor-manager Anew McMaster and his wife Marjorie Wilmore, who had just founded the touring company which they ran until the late 1950s. Christopher's godparents were Ivor Novello and Constance Collier.

He was one of few actors actually born in that proverbially invoked maternity ward of the theatrical profession, the property-basket. He was carried on stage in several productions in which babies were preferred to the customary bundles of cloth, but made his first important appearance at the age of seven at the Shakespeare Memorial Theatre, Stratford-upon-Avon, as Marcius, son of Coriolanus, his father having been engaged as the principal actor for the 1933 season.

He was sent to Glenstal Abbey school in County Limerick, performing with the family company during the holidays. He continued to act after leaving school — reluctantly, as some of his contemporaries would have it, and because it was "the only profession he knew".

He adapted 19th-century novels for the stage, and directed the modern plays which supplemented the McMasters' largely Shakespearian repertoire. A peculiarly childlike relish and absorption informed both his acting and writing. His earliest leading role in the West End was in Saroyan's *The Beautiful People* in 1948. He often appeared at the Dublin Gate Theatre for Hilton Edwards and his uncle, Micheál MacLiammóir. A now elderly theatregoing generation will recall his marvellous Fool in *King Lear* at the Gaiety Theatre; this casting may have been a metaphor for his own life in the 1950s — always overshadowed by his father in the name part.

It seems that Christopher McMaster, though no stranger to eccentricities himself, sought a more conventional lifestyle than that of the touring *artiste*. He enrolled in a BBC training course in 1956, and was soon directing the *Starr* series on television. He moved to Granada TV at a time of great expansion in the industry, and there directed many plays and serials, including over sixty of the early episodes of *Coronation Street*.

Moving to Southern Television in 1967, he became head of children's programmes, where, it would seem, free rein was given to his quirky imagination. His serial *Freewheelers* ran to 96 instalments, and was seen all over the world. Other series followed, among them *Rogue's Rock*, *Park Ranger*, *The Ravelled Thread*, *Scarf Jack* and *Midnight is a Place* — the latter nominated for BAFTA award. During the 1980s he worked in a freelance capacity for Disney and other companies in Hollywood.

Christopher McMaster is survived by his wife, Jill Gotts, by his two sons, Paul and John, and by his sister, the actress Mary Rose McMaster, who now lives in California.

C.F.

19 Obituary of Christopher McMaster by Christopher Fitz-Simon

14 – Chiswick

Stratford had not been an especially happy time for Mac but it was a large feather in his cap professionally, he'd earned a good salary and paid some old bills, and though not exactly a family man, at least regarding Chris and me, we'd all been together for six months in one place and it must have given him a feeling of security. However, he'd decided, as only Mac could, to turn against it and that was that.

Not long after the Stratford season, Sir Oswald Stoll, who had seen the plays at Stratford, invited Mac with his own company to do a season of Shakespeare at the Chiswick Empire Theatre in London. Sir Oswald was an impresario who had successfully produced commercial theatre for years and who now wanted to do Shakespeare, not an isolated production as done in the West End, but in repertory, over several weeks. This came about after Sir Oswald had invited the Stratford Company to come with the same repertory of plays done that season. But the management refused, as they wanted to keep the festival exclusively at Stratford.

Mac was second choice but he was pleased at being asked and agreed enthusiastically. He gathered the company together and invited several London actors to join him as well as a couple from Stratford. He was once more in his stride, answerable only to himself.

A man after Mac's heart, the combination of Sir Oswald the showman and Mac, the Shakespearean actor-manager was a very exciting union. I think my father was probably more in his element at this time than at any other in his life. He loved touring Ireland, but this had the added ingredient and excitement of being in London, his early stomping ground and the city that is the ambition of most actors to play in. It was just what he needed after feeling 'persecuted' at Stratford.

The plays to be done were all ones Mac had done for the last seven or eight years on tour. No anxiety and agony of learning new lines! He would be doing what he knew best but on a larger, grander scale.

So we packed up in Loxley and moved to London. The flat in George Street had been finally let go during the lean times of weekly rep. Now my parents leased a large flat in Chelsea; Fernshaw House, Fernshaw Road S.W.10. I remember it well. I even remember that Flaxman 9837 was the telephone number!

It was light and spacious with a little walled garden at the back and a tiny lawn that my mother cut with nail scissors! Chris and I were there only on holidays from school, but our visits were long enough to have left an impression. We didn't have a house or even a flat in Ireland, so Fernshaw became the first home for Chris and me.

The sitting room was large, ornate, and comfortable, filled with the treasures Mac had collected on his travels. A decorator would have found it to be a jumble of no particular style or period. A red lacquered Chinese cabinet stood next to a guilt and tapestry settee and chairs of the 18th century. A carved mahogany Buddha was beside a reproduction of a Fra Angelico, and a delicate crystal chandelier looked down on a pair of rough brightly painted wooden candle sticks. There was the beautiful 18th century screen of carved guilt and needlepoint. These things were real and valuable, not props, and most had been on the stage at one time or another. I wonder sometimes what became of these beautiful things; Mana had sold some of them towards the end of her life. I have the screen but it would be out of place in my redwood cottage in California, so it stays permanently with friends in Carlow.

The sitting room at Fernshaw was reflective of my father's character, colourful, theatrical, humorous and dramatic and a little childlike too. These things were his toys, acquired in his bouts of 'squandermania' and always with an eye to putting them on stage.

The dining room was more conventional, a study in beautiful highly polished dark wood and, on the wall, two large pictures in lacquered frames of Rachel, the French actress of the early 19th century, the other of Mrs Siddons. There was a cabinet filled with Venetian glass, and on the floor the black carpet that was the reason for my parents getting married!

For several years before the war and in between tours and various seasons, Fernshaw became quite a meeting place. I remember Ivor Novello and Bobbie Andrews 'popping in' and the musical comedy actress Evelyn Laye, and her husband Frank Lawton, who played David Copperfield, as a man, in the film that starred Freddie Bartholomew, and Noël Coward and his entourage, Constance Collier, the mysterious 'sphinx-like creature' as Micheál called her, and of course, Micheál and Hilton when they were in London.

Chris and I were still supposed to be seen and not heard, and not even seen or be in the same room if the conversation turned to sex and gossip. We hid sometimes behind the aforementioned screen and didn't dare breathe; we didn't know that our feet and ankles were in full view because the screen had little legs that lifted it off the floor. Once when Daddy knew we were there, he said in a loud voice full of parental authority: 'Mary-Rose must go at once to a new boarding school, a strict one where they rap her knuckles when she gets out of hand.' And Chris, who could do no wrong because he was so clever, was to be taken on a trip to Italy to 'broaden his education.'

I had a tantrum at once. I seemed to be fond of kicking and screaming in those days, and poor Mana, who had to try to explain it was just a silly joke, was at her wits' end. I remember her crying and saying she didn't know what to do with me, and the more she cried the more frantic I became. I was afraid one day she'd not be able to deal with me and give me away!

As I grew older the tantrums stopped and instead I became very shy. I was told I was a 'shadow' by the late Carolyn Swift who, with her husband Alan Simpson, ran the little Pike Theatre Club in Dublin. 'You hardly spoke so it was difficult to know you,' she said. However, there were, I think, quite reasonable reasons for my shyness, but I need to get back to Mac and the season at Chiswick.

The Chiswick Empire Theatre was not in the West End but in the Borough of Chiswick, one of the many self-contained districts that make up the city of London. It was a huge house seating 2,500 people and better known for music hall and variety shows than for serious drama. Mac wasn't daunted. He'd wanted to take on the Tivoli in Dublin after all. The idea of attracting large audiences at reasonable prices had always appealed to him, besides he could hardly pass up the opportunity to do *Othello* and *Hamlet* for the first time in London. The other plays included *The Shrew*, *The Merchant*, *Richard II*, *As You Like It*, and *Macbeth*.

The season opened with *The Shrew*, and if any of the old variety audiences came, they must have been delighted, for Mac had directed it to attract them ' ... in a rambunctious, boisterous, and full of fun production' as one critic remarked '... here is proof once and for all that Shakespeare is not highbrow, remote, and otherworldly.' Something that Mac knew all along!

When Othello opened, Darlington of the *Daily Telegraph* wrote that (Mac's) '... performance had vigour but no subtlety and hardly any poetry.' This is curious because I'd say quite the opposite is true. He had a natural ear for poetry. Didn't one critic say of his Romeo that 'he was at least as much in love with the lovely words as he was with Juliet.' The incredible range of Mac's voice made him naturally poetic. When he was tired in later years, or if the house was bad, he'd 'send on technique' as he called it and some words would come out 'sing songy' but one could never say it was not poetic, he was too influenced by the lyricism of Verdi and Puccini not to have been.

The season at the Chiswick Empire was ultimately successful in spite of 'patchy' reviews. The houses were full and Sir Oswald was pleased and asked Mac to play the lead in a play called *The Golden Toy*, but he said 'no.' The pressure of doing six demanding parts in less than a month and immediately after the long and difficult season at Stratford had exhausted him. He retreated back to Ireland. The one place where he could do as he pleased always, where he felt calm and un-pressured, and much as he loved the excitement of the London Theatre scene, his peace of mind was more important.

Mac went to stay with the Flemings in New Ross in county Wexford, dear friends and great admirers. I've sometimes wondered about him and the Flemings' attractive daughter! It's difficult to say, but again, I was too young to know and such things were never spoken of.

Mana meanwhile was still in London, left as usual to tie up the loose ends of the Chiswick season. Chris and I had gone to stay with Aunt Peg (the scattty Aunt) who, with her artist husband, lived at the time in Chiswick. Our cousins David and Moira were both a little older than us and I remember thinking how English they were. Well spoken, well mannered, and in the process of being well educated.

They lived in a well-ordered house where, in spite of Aunt Peg's scattiness, meals and daily rituals were always on time (probably because Aunt Peg had a housekeeper and two maids). I envied our cousins. I'm not sure what is special about a routine life, it could be rather dull, but the idea was appealing at the time. I longed for an ordinary life like theirs, but that was not in the cards, indeed it was to become more changeable as Chris and I grew older.

Mana eventually went back to Ireland to organize a new tour. Chris went back to Exeter and I to Lancing and we'd join the company in the holidays. This was our routine. We both went on the stage when needed. Chris, agreeably; I, under protest. Daddy put on *Little Lord Fauntleroy* for Chris, and he played one of the witches in *Macbeth*, and I was a page and there to fill out a crowd scene, but as yet I'd not spoken a word on the stage.

When Chris was eleven or twelve, he played Michael in *Peter Pan* (the part Micheál had played as a boy) at the Palladium Theatre in London, a huge auditorium, more suited for musicals as it is today, than for *Peter Pan*, but its star Anna Neagle, was a well-known film actress at the time and the public as always was intrigued to see a film star 'in the flesh.' I remember Chris wore a bulky harness under his pyjamas and flying – actually swinging like a pendulum – from one side of the stage to the other, and how he had to hold tight to a little doll unaccountably attached to the wall above the mantelpiece to stop himself from swinging back again. Odd how these small things stay in one's mind.

Around the time of *Peter Pan*, Chris made a film called *Scruffy*, a sentimental tale of an orphan boy and his dog. He was becoming quite a seasoned actor. If he'd been ambitious for himself (a strangely missing characteristic it seems in most of my family) or had a stage mother pushing him, there's little doubt he'd have become as sought after as Micheál had been in his young days. Chris' quality of innocence was very appealing and his total lack of self-consciousness, but acting wasn't important to him, he did it because he'd been born into a theatrical family and it was expected of him.

It was expected of me too, but I wonder sometimes if I was temperamentally suited to be an actress. I became quite a good one (I had a marvellous teacher, who taught by example rather than instruction) and the theatre was in my blood and bones, but my shyness and fearfulness persecuted me, and I was not comfortable with the bright assured people it attracted. I admired them, even secretly wished I could be like them, but I was not.

15 – Religion, Scotland, and Pneumonia

Chris and I were now around nine and ten years old and we were spending more time on tour and less at school. That is – I was. Neither Mac nor Mana thought schooling had any great value, much better that we should learn 'the business', but Chris being the brainy one needed and wanted to go to school, and he insisted that he at least complete preparatory school. He was a born student, his mind was inquiring and dying for knowledge. I was the opposite; I was lazy-minded like my father, and being on tour was much better than going back to school, even Lancing and Mrs Old.

It was discussed briefly that I should go to a convent in Arklow, but I said definitely 'no' and the matter was never spoken of again. I feel sorry now that I didn't go. I believe it would have given me the solid grounding I needed, set me up academically and spiritually, and I needed spirituality in my life. Ireland was then 90% Catholic, and it was natural that I should gravitate towards the Catholic Church and I did wherever we were on tour and even at Lancing. It became the solid unchangeable force in my life, I loved God, but what did I know about Him or the church? My faith was truly blind.

Spirituality was hardly discussed in my family and I was thought of as 'wanting' by Mac in my practice of it. His attitude was humorously mocking, but I'd never know and I can only surmise what rumblings were going on deep inside of him. I've found for many people faith is something private and not communicated to anyone, so it may have been for my father. Outwardly, his 'faith' was completely theatrical. He'd sometimes dress in one of his lovely Saville Row suits, and go to Mass a few minutes late to make sure that his entrance had registered with the citizenry of the town. 'Good for business!' he said, and he'd carry a rosary and genuflect to the floor! If this sounds hypocritical, I don't think so because he wasn't opposed to the church; far from it. I think he'd love to have had deep genuine faith but as far as I could tell, it wasn't there. As it was, he was impressed by the outward trappings of the church: the incense, the music, the rich colourful vestments, the processions – he loved it all; there was terrific theatrical value in it!

As for my mother, I never remember her going inside a church. Her background had been non-religious and the name Jesus Christ didn't seem to be in her vocabulary. But I often wonder if she didn't acknowledge the creator of all things, as she was much too thoughtful not to and had a side to her that none of us, not even Mac, was privy to. Perhaps if I'd known her better in her old age (but I wasn't there and I regret it) I'd have discovered more about her private side. She was often remote to me only showing what she wanted us to know, as if she were protecting her inner thoughts. My brother Chris dutifully accepted the teachings of the Church, being a student of two Catholic schools, but he didn't practice Catholicism when he was on tour with us, and later he became quite indifferent to it.

It isn't difficult in a theatre company not to give much consideration to a deity in whatever form it takes. Most theatre people are 'free spirits' and our company was no different. In fact, they were inclined to make fun of the extreme piety of the townspeople about whom Micheál once said, 'The Irish people were never meant to be Christians because their faith is rooted in superstition dating back to the pagan and druid times.'

One further observation on religion in Ireland: Mac genuinely respected 'people of the cloth'. Indeed, Catholic nuns and priests all around the country were his good friends and they were some of the most enthusiastic theatre goers, but it was more than just that; he was impressed by their devotion and their theological knowledge and he knew too that they admired him! He was also impressed by the hierarchy of the church, towards bishops he was respectful and quite formal, with the archbishop of Tuam, who was a close friend, he was the epitome of humility, bowing and kissing his ring and backing out of the room as with royalty. Yes, it was partly an act, but if he'd not had some genuine admiration for them, he'd not have done it.

The next three years were mostly spent in Ireland but in 1937 the company went to Bournemouth in the South of England to do a six-month season of weekly rep. Mac must have felt the need to do penance for his sins to have agreed. Why would he put himself through such agony again? But as I later realized, taking the odd season in England where Mac and the company were guaranteed an agreed amount was necessary, as touring Ireland, however good business was, it didn't always meet expenses. It should be noted that my parents never solicited backers, nor did they ever receive grants from the government. The company was always self-sustaining but touring Ireland was never a money-making venture.

Bournemouth I suppose was necessary for survival but it was not good for my father's well-being. With the usual drama he saw in every situation, he announced that he was '... reduced to being (if temporarily) a bloody weekly rep. actor again and there's hardly anything more depressing than that.' However, towards the end of the six months at Bournemouth, Mac had had enough and ended the season abruptly before the appointed time, but instead of returning home, Mac decided to accept another, though less demanding engagement in Scotland and off we all went to the Presbyterian stronghold of Dundee.

The Alhambra Theatre was a large granite building in the heart of a not very attractive city, and we drove back and forth across the famous Tay Bridge each day to the small town of Broughty Ferry where we had digs and where I immediately became ill with pneumonia. Mac was always sympathetic when anyone in the family was ill, especially towards my mother.

I lay for two days on the mat in front of the fire, unable or unwilling to move. I'd a high temperature and all I wanted was to stay there and not move. Mac brought me special things to eat and drink and one day he came in with a Monopoly game, new at the time and quite expensive, which neither he nor I ever learned to play! The pneumonia went through its phases and with antibiotics not yet invented, my parents watched anxiously as I went through the 'crisis.' I did get through it as is evident, but it left me with a pair of weak lungs and a perpetual cough. I still remember the stingy landlady who brought me plates of bread, fried in dripping and cut into strips which she called 'savoury fingers.'

Dundee was, for me, dark, gray and forbidding, but I was eleven years old and sick, and it's probably nothing of the sort. We must have done fairly well there because Mac and the company were invited to return the next year and they did, but I didn't. Mana must have decided a little more schooling would be a good thing and I went back to Lancing for what was to be the last year of my 'formal' education.

The second season at the Alhambra included *Hamlet* and *Othello*. Mac felt that the Scots would appreciate Shakespeare being akin to the Irish Celts, and they played to generally good houses. Bournemouth and Dundee had been worthwhile and they had paid some Irish bills but it was a depressing time for Mac and he couldn't wait to get back to the Irish countryside but first he would make one more exciting trip outside Ireland, just in time, as the rumblings of war were becoming serious.

Micheál and Hilton had arranged a tour of Egypt produced by the British Arts Council and invited Mac to play Othello, Malvolio in *Twelfth Night* and Jack Worthing in *The Importance of Being Earnest*.

Mac was naturally delighted and even more so when several of his actors including Walter Humphries were also invited. A few weeks in the Egyptian sun before going back on tour was just what he needed. The Egyptian visit was in every way a happy successful adventure and what a wondrous memory to have before war would put us all in a new grey world.

In Cairo, the company played at the Opera House where the first ever production of *Aida* was done. King Farouk and his entourage came to the opening and he presented Mac with a large scarab which he wore around his neck as Othello for years to come.

The British Ambassador fêted the company with garden parties and receptions. They visited the bazaars where of course Mac went mad again with 'squandermania', but in spite of the excitement of it all, Mac didn't function well without his alter ego, and he sent for Mana, who had been to Egypt and the Holy Land before in the days of 'Daddy' Perrin and his family. She had wonderful memories of it and jumped at the chance of going back. It seems odd that she wasn't included in the first place and she may have been, but she always put Mac's interests before her own and when Mac was away from the usual routine of touring, she felt she was needed to keep things running at home.

From Cairo the company went to Alexandria and finally to Valetta in Malta where they played to packed houses in the Opera House, later bombed to pieces by Mussolini.

At the end of the tour Mac took off with Walter, Micheál, and Hilton for a holiday in Tunis and wound up in Paris and London. My mother wasn't invited. It wasn't unusual at all for Mac to go off like this with close friends and Mana didn't seem to mind at all. Most wives, I'm sure, would have felt left out and be quite offended. Not Mana, she knew she was important to Mac. She knew too that there was a side to my father that liked to be with men, cronies who enjoyed the same childish stories and jokes. They could stay up 'til morning, go swimming at night, eat at exotic restaurants, and go to endless opera and theatre performances, and she had no quarrel with this.

Encouraged by the Egyptian tour Mac sent Walter off to India to arrange a tour there for his company, which he did, and he wrote later to Mac saying he'd booked the first three months and that he thought it was going to be rewarding and fun; but World War II was by now more than a threat, it was imminent. Travel to the East was stopped, and the intended tour was cancelled.

My parents went back to the neutrality of Ireland. Christopher was already there, a boarder at the Benedictine School of Glenstal in county Limerick. I was still at Lancing.

In the summer of 1938 Hitler marched into Poland. Chamberlain went to Germany for talks and when he returned he said in the famous broadcast that 'There would be peace in our time,' but only weeks later he returned once again from a meeting with Hitler and announced that 'Talks had broken down and consequently a state of war exits between our two countries.'

I remember that day, we were all glued to the little radio, arched, shaped like a cathedral window in Mrs Old's sitting room and I can still see the strained look on her face wondering, I'm sure, when she would see her only son again who was an engineer in the Anglo Iranian Oil Company. My very dear aunt, who always made everything seem alright, looked suddenly severe. The security I'd always felt with her was suddenly threatened and I was frightened. The usual reserve of the British vanished as strangers in the street talked in muffled tones to one another; I was sure it was about me, a conspiracy was being hatched to send me away somewhere!

Of course there was no conspiracy but I was going away. Overnight, plans were made for me to go home. I didn't know the seriousness of what was happening, I just knew a huge upheaval was going on and it was different from all the other changes in my life, there was more finality, a feeling of no turning back. Would I ever go back to Lancing and Aunt Doff? What was ahead? Would I go to school in Ireland? Would I join the company and have to act whether I wanted to or not? No decision had to be made, for quite naturally at the age of twelve, I became a permanent member of my father's company.

16 – Loughleven Cottage

Mac and Mana had reluctantly given up the Fernshaw flat. It had been their haven, a safe place to rest. Now it was gone and it was the end too, though they probably didn't know it at the time, of the ties that had kept them connected with the English theatre.

The family needed to find a home, a permanent one in Ireland, and it seemed natural to gravitate towards Howth, a place special to Micheál, and Aunt Craven still lived there. Mana too had a nostalgic fondness for it, it reminded her of Micheál in his early 20s and Máire and the young exploring years.

We found a whitewashed cottage sitting on the top of a cliff near the old Baily Lighthouse with glorious views of the Dublin mountains and Wicklow in the distance. Loughleven Cottage was solid and old and primitive. It had no running water or electricity and I loved it at once; it was home; completely and forever. This simple little place that had once served teas to hikers became the unlikely repository of the furnishings and treasures of the Chelsea flat. Could anything be more incongruous or theatrical?

Since Loughleven had at one time been two cottages joined together, it was decided to take down a wall and make the sitting room twice as large. It must have been quite a shock for an unknowing visitor to open the door and find himself in a Salon of the 18th century.

The large kitchen, the natural gathering place, was the warmest room in the cottage, having an enormous cast iron range, for which we had to find kindling before we could have a cup of tea in the morning. This was transformed with the famous black carpet, the beautiful mahogany gate-legged table (that mysteriously disappeared after my mother died) the high backed

Dutch chairs with seats of needlepoint, and on the thick whitewashed walls were hung the portraits of Mrs Siddons and Rachel, McCready, Kean, and the divine Sarah. It was a fascinating blending of sophistication and simplicity.

But there were the difficulties of no 'modern conveniences' that most of us take for granted. We had to go through gorse bushes almost to the top of the cliff to draw drinking water from the well. The oil lamps smoked and didn't give off enough light. We'd walk from room to room with candles that dripped on the furniture and the carpets. Heating water for a bath was a major ordeal. A large copper cylinder stood next to the range in the kitchen and was supposed to be fed by a storage tank of rainwater in the backyard. I remember the tadpoles and other little creatures swimming around in it. The problem was that if too many people had recently used it and the tank was empty, the cylinder was in danger of exploding.

Those things were entirely unimportant to me. I loved Loughleven Cottage with all my heart but we were not to see it very often during the four years of the war when one tour evolved into another and we'd go home only for Christmas and Holy Week and snatch a week here and there in the summer, a total of perhaps six weeks out of a year.

Soon after we moved to the cottage I was allowed to have a dog, something I'd always wanted. I named him Bran after the warrior Finn McCool's great wolfhound, which my Bran certainly was not; I doubt that his mother knew who his father was! I also had two cats, Delilah-puss, and Debussy-cat. I was in Heaven. I had all I ever wanted. This is what I had dreamed of and always when it was time to go back on tour I wanted to die, and once I nearly did! The only time I saw my father in a raging temper was when I ran away and hid in the gorse bushes halfway down a cliff in the hope I'd not be found and not have to go back on tour.

My poor little mother was crying and was sure I had flung myself into the sea. When I did reappear after almost the whole night, Daddy was spitting fire, 'How dare you upset your mother like this', he shouted. 'There's no excuse, I don't want to see you or think about you ever again,' and he took up a skirt I was making and tore it to pieces. 'Mac,' pleaded my mother, 'she's unhappy, try to understand.' I think my father was more put out that he was suddenly expected to behave like a father than anything else; it was a role he'd never studied. I suppose because this was such an unusual occurrence I remember what my father said, word for word. This little episode didn't do much good for my shaky health, and I had to go to bed for several days with a temperature of 102.

A few years ago my younger son David and I visited Howth and the clump of bushes where the cottage used to be. Demolished now for many years so that the natural loveliness of the hills and cliffs of Howth would not be disfigured by a crumbling old cottage.

We picked our way into the bushes to see if we could find any evidence of a house ever being there. I pointed out to David where the kitchen had been and his grandparents' room, and the 'big sitting room' as we called it.

David was on all fours as he hunted around the undergrowth for something, anything, then suddenly he stood up holding a small handful of broken slates from the roof. He handed me one of the largest and said I should take it home with me. Home? This darling cottage was my home and would be forever, or so I thought, but now it's long gone and David was a tangible reminder of my very different life in California and of all the in-between years. It seemed like a fantasy that the cottage ever existed, but it did and I have a little piece of grey slate to prove it.

17 - Touring during the War

The war had begun and we felt the effects almost at once. There would be no more jaunts outside Ireland and the need to keep going all year long meant going to almost every small town and village in the country. There would be split weeks, twice as much packing and unpacking, and looking for digs. A reduced company, difficulties in getting material for costumes and replacing scenery, and for Mac the worst was not being able to buy new lighting equipment from London.

Now suddenly at the age of twelve and a half, I was an apprentice in the company and I was surely the most unlikely one the theatre had ever had. I went to work right away helping with the costumes and props and generally running errands. Now it was time to begin playing small parts! The idea of walking on the stage, even 'heavily disguised' and actually having to speak, filled me with horror. I thought if I hid behind the flats during rehearsal I'd not be noticed but then I'd hear my name being called in a loud authoritative voice and there was no way out. Mac said, 'She can do Fleance, Chris is more useful as a witch.' And so I played Banquo's son in *Macbeth* for the first time with unfortunate results. 'How goes the night boy?' asks Banquo. 'The moon is down, I have not heard the clock,' was my line but I couldn't say it because I'd caught sight of the audience and was instantly paralyzed. My voice trailed off after the first couple of words and became inaudible. Banquo quickly came in with 'And she goes down at twelve.' 'I take 'tis later Sir, 'was my next and only other line, but nothing came out! I stood there glued to the spot unable to say a word, my mouth wide open. 'Hopeless,' muttered my father, 'what's to be done with her.' 'Nothing' said my mother, 'She's just shy, she'll learn.'

This kind of thing made me feel hopelessly inadequate. I wanted so much to please my father, but once on the stage I wasn't in control. I couldn't think, I couldn't move, my legs shook, and I wanted to 'relieve exhausted nature' as Chris called it. He added to my insecurities too because he was always so calm. I have no idea why I had such difficulties with a simple thing as saying a few lines. 'Made a nice mess of that, didn't you Mary-Rose', he'd say, and I'd wish I was dead or at least back in the days of Williamstown. What terrible thing was I afraid of? Was it just my shyness? Why was the audience of friendly accepting people so intimidating? I've never explained it.

Touring Ireland in the war years was uncomfortable and damp and why we didn't all die of pneumonia is a mystery. Soon rationing of all imported goods began, but for a time Mac managed to keep 'the royal car' running by knowing the right people to supply him with just enough petrol. My mother travelled in it and the leading ladies and Eugene, the character actor, and of course Mac who drove – if you could call it that. He did sit behind the wheel and steer, the gears were things you moved about if you felt like it, but he had no idea of their function, and some of the time he focused on the road but it wasn't important. Mana was a necessary backseat driver, and thank goodness, for Mac's mind was always far away.

Arriving in a 'new town' was a small endurance test for me; I felt nomadic. Everyone helped unload the lorry except Mac, and Eugene who was too elderly, and the leading ladies who were too grand. The rest of us trudged in and out of the hall, with boxes of electrics, music equipment, huge hampers of costumes, furniture, batons, and flats. Chris managed quite often to avoid doing it. He just wasn't to be seen.

After this was done, it was time to look for digs. The seasoned actors kept records of past digs and noted if they had been 'possible,' how much they had paid for them, and wrote beside an address something like, 'dreary but clean, filthy food, charming landlady.' Looking for digs was hard and I usually attached myself to one of the women who didn't mind asking, 'Do you have accommodation?' (I thought it was very bold to knock on the door of a person's private house and expect to be put up.)

What a relief when we were settled; at least we had a home for a few days even if not the best. Digs were seldom comfortable, they were quite often horrible in fact, but the landladies were wonderful, cheerful, kind, and so poor. How well I remember the cold, hard beds, and the legions of fleas that did somersaults when you turned the bedclothes down. The bare sitting room where we ate a steady diet of black pudding and greasy rashers and eggs, and the one turf fire we huddled around, the heat making curious mottled patterns on the front of one's legs. How is it possible that Colm O'Doherty, an ex-actor now living in Australia writes: 'They were golden days, the best of my life.'

Mac added to the repertory with a few more 'frightful' plays like, *The Shop at Sly Corner* and *Ten Little Indians*. I'm not sure why he did them other than to give himself a night off. The country audiences had always shown a preference for the classics, so it wasn't for their popular appeal. Perhaps it was Mac's way of showing that he could be modern or that he needed to compete with the cinema.

Those were the plays he hardly gave any thought to and they practically directed themselves. Mac would work out the moves and give a general idea of what was needed and then wander away in the middle of rehearsal, bored and detached. I can still hear Mana, as she did quite often, quietly reprimanding him 'Mac, go back at once, you cannot leave everyone stranded.'

Now with only seven or eight actors in the company including the stage manager and the electrician covering all the parts in Shakespeare, it was like watching a magician at work, as an actor would exit as Rosencrantz and enter ten seconds later as one of the players. It was a challenge, a race to see how quickly the transformation could be done.

The company never seemed to be cast down by the bedraggled conditions of touring during the war. They made jokes about the fleas and the greasy food, and they were grateful to have digs where the lavatory was in the house and not down a path at the end of the garden! The work was relentless and the physical conditions not good, but the company seemed to be stimulated by it all. I have no memories of the actors complaining or being depressed. But we weren't angels either, naturally sometimes tempers flared. I remember Harold Pinter in a later tour being white with rage because someone had moved his make-up and put their own in its place. 'Where the fucking hell is my god damned make-up,' he yelled. 'I'll disembowel the bastard, tear his bloody guts out!' Just sound and fury; actors like the sound of their own voices.

Naturally the bad economy in Ireland during this time affected the financial well-being of the company. Unemployment was rampant and many, especially the younger people, simply had no money for the theatre. The company had to go on shares, but the shares usually came to about the same as their salaries which was about six pounds a week. Unbelievable as it sounds, it was quite average for the time. The Abbey Theatre actors were making about the same and when the young Orson Welles joined Micheál and Hilton at the Gate, he was paid three pounds a week!

We sometimes played as many as three matinees a week in convents and colleges to keep afloat. These were done for a guaranteed fee, and how we loved it when the company was invited to a wonderful meal afterwards, all laid out in very grand dining rooms with beautiful lace tablecloths and antique silver and the nuns with their flushed cheeks and beautiful skin fluttering around us. Mana said their high colour was sometimes an indication that they had tuberculosis. Many people in Ireland at this time suffered with lung diseases of various kinds and the hospitals were full.

It was a 'thin time' as Mana called it for the theatre everywhere. The theatres in London were mostly closed 'for the duration' and many well-known actors put on uniforms and joined ENSA, the organization formed by the British Arts Council to entertain the troops abroad.

In Dublin, the larger theatres were barely staggering along, with no touring companies coming from England, they had to rely entirely on homegrown productions. This turned out to be a healthy time of growth for the Irish theatre and many little groups sprung up, like the Pike Theatre Club and the Eblana. Micheál and Hilton were feeling the pinch but kept on going with small cast plays at the Gate. And before the war, where our company had gone to the larger towns and played in reasonably well equipped theatres and town halls, now we went to every grey little town in the country and played in cinemas, scout and temperance halls, school auditoriums, and even a boathouse. Anywhere there was room for an audience and with luck – a stage!

The price of tickets then was two and six, two shillings, one and three and six pence (saying it had a sort of rhythm.) Low, even for those days, but still too much for the clutches of little boys with runny noses and bare feet who hung around the box-office. 'Will you give us a pass for the play missus?' They'd ask my mother. At eight or nine years old one could wonder how they could be interested in *Hamlet* or *A Tale of Two Cities*, but it wasn't often they had such excitement. The 'play crowd' was in town and we were a curiosity, besides we were real people even if we were a bit peculiar and that was better than going to the 'fillums' where the people might be dead even – because it was only a moving picture. I had a special feeling for those children with their weathered little faces and a kind of innocent wile that helped them survive for they had about them such spirit and good humour – and a bit of the devil – one could almost envy them.

I hated it when our company was called the 'fit-ups' which to me described the broken down little groups that travelled the country in dilapidated caravans doing one-night stands in the tiniest of villages. They did potted versions of *East Lynn* and *The Drunkard* in front of a backdrop that had furniture and flowers painted on it. They were the 'fit-ups' – not us! How could we be thought of in the same way with our beautiful costumes and special lighting effects? But we were, because all the term means is that because of the lack of amenities in some halls, everything had to be 'fitted up' and this we did quite often. But I still wince when someone says 'You did the fit-ups didn't you, all over Ireland?'

If this life we led on tour was hard and the conditions primitive, it wasn't important. Nowadays, I look back on those years and smile. There was wonder in turning a dingy old hall into a colourful playhouse, the sense of accomplishment we felt in making something out of very little; the wonder of the kind and perceptive people of the towns, the audience. Virgin territory as my father had said, unsophisticated yes, un-intellectual perhaps, but always enthusiastic and responsive. I think of the glory of the Irish countryside with the coming of Spring, and walks in the afternoons, and every bank and roadside covered with primroses and violets, and the tiny fields full of all kinds of baby animals. Memories of hot cups of tea the kind landladies always had ready as we walked in the door, and the camaraderie amongst the actors who, by the nature of our constant moving, were each other's closest friends. Some became 'coupled and inseparable,' a natural condition in theatre companies, and though I baulked at the continual changes growing up, in a strange way there was consistency in the endless moving that was comforting. For the routine of the company hardly changed from the time of its inception to the last tour in 1955.

Not the least of the wonder was the repertory done by the company at any given time. Shakespeare, Sheridan, Goldsmith, Wilde, and Sophocles, a handful of frightful plays and melodramas, but Shakespeare was always at the core and always and forever, *Othello, Hamlet, Macbeth, The Merchant of Venice, As You Like It, The Taming of the Shrew*, and later *King Lear*. How was it possible that those of us who were in the company for many years were not completely weary of them? For the same reason that one can never be tired of Wagner, Verdi or Puccini, the poetry of Yeats or the symphonies of Beethoven.

Some years ago, I visited Shamus Locke, an actor in the company in the forties. Retired now and living in splendour in Southern California, I asked him about the time he spent touring with Mac. 'Well, it was without doubt the happiest time of my life,' he said, 'and nothing that I've done in the theatre afterwards' (he later became well known in the musical theatre in London) 'has made such an impression. One had to be ready and alert to play three or four parts in ten plays all the time. The experience of learning how to build a stage if necessary, rig the lighting, look after the props, the music, the scenery, the costumes, and play every kind of part in all these plays pushed everyone's intellectual and physical capacities to the limit, and it was something never to be forgotten or lived again.' And to quote Harold Pinter: 'The whole thing was one of learning – something about how to live and, for me, this period (with Mac) in fact represented the Golden Age!'

18– Lord Longford and Oedipus

While he was crisscrossing our tiny country unrelentingly during the war, Micheál and Hilton were having their own difficulties in Dublin.

The Gate Theatre, though now firmly established and greatly admired, was always in need of funds and in the late 1930s they had grudgingly agreed to share the theatre with Lord Longford, who had bailed them out more than once in the past.

Lord Edward Longford was a patron of the arts and a classical scholar. He formed his own company, Longford Productions, and leased the Gate six months of the year relieving 'the boys' of the grind of producing play after play and providing them with some income. They were also free to accept engagements with other companies. It seemed to be a very practical arrangement, but Micheál and Hilton resented the whole thing, dismissed Lord Longford as a wealthy dilettante and spoke disparagingly of his productions and his choice of plays. 'Biting the hand that feeds them,' Mac had said. The truth is that it's unlikely that Micheál and Hilton could have kept going if not for Lord Longford.

The rivalry between the two companies was, I suppose, natural and it was natural for me to feel a kinship with Micheál and Hilton, whose productions were alive and exciting. The Longfords were dull, efficient, professional and workmanlike, but lacking .... what? The inventiveness of Hilton as a director, and the star quality and artistry of Micheál?

The financial woes of the Gate were unavoidable with a capacity of only 400. The price of admission, though higher than ours, was low by London standards and even playing to full houses, it wasn't always possible to meet expenses. In spite of this, the productions were always lavish and beautifully costumed, and Micheál and Hilton lived quite opulently.

After leaving their large flat on the top floor of a building in Dawson Street, they bought a spacious early Victorian house in Harcourt Terrace, a quiet neighbourhood near the canal. I've no idea how they financed it, but they had some wealthy and influential friends who probably helped. They filled it with colourful furniture, and thousands of books. There was an office on the ground floor and a full-time business manager and secretary.

Cooks came and went and sometimes the valet would double as a cook. Harcourt Terrace was always crowded with people; actors being interviewed, doctors, solicitors, friends of all kinds, including film and stage actors of note who were working in Dublin at the time. Once when I was visiting, Peter Ustinov was just leaving. He spoke such good English I thought, and he said to me 'You live in this charming quaint little city do you, how lucky you are!' If he knew how seldom I saw it.

When I was 'home' for a time (as I was once when I rebelled against touring and went to a secretarial school in Dublin) Micheál always invited me to lunch on Tuesdays together with Aunt Craven who was now living in Dublin, and Cousin Sally Travers. Sally was the daughter of Aunt Christine, (the one who died after supposedly being bitten by a monkey). Lunches were always entertaining and sometimes quite bizarre. Served on an antique mahogany table in a formal dining room, everything was laid very correctly and the valet of the time would enter with a tray and serve each guest on the left. It all appeared to be the very height of gracious living until you looked a little closer and found the table was sticky from the last meal and the forks and knives needed an extra rinse or two. The food was usually exotic, Indian curry or Japanese sushi; and then ... how well I remember the day Micheál and Hilton had one of their shouting rows, right there in front of Sally, me, and poor Aunt Craven; that is Hilton did the shouting and Micheál, forever the martyr, sat silent and wounded. Eventually Hilton could stand it no longer, his anger subsided and he became very calm, he sat down and quietly and methodically picked up every piece of silver on the table and threw it on the floor, and then the plates and the glasses – everything that was on the table. No one interfered, not Micheál and certainly not us. Aunt Craven sat stoically, her mouth set in a hard line of disapproval. Tommy, the valet stood by the door with enormous tears rolling down his cheeks; I'm not sure why, he'd surely witnessed this kind of thing many times before.

I was sorry for Micheál. What a bombastic ogre Hilton was. Sometimes when I was visiting, he'd storm about shouting at Micheál, or he'd be sarcastic which had more bite. Years later I realized that Micheál was not faultless. He needled Hilton, and he could be just as sarcastic – and with far more eloquence and finesse. He didn't raise his voice as Hilton did, but his words could be deadly.

The Gate Theatre, even with its physical limitations and impracticability was for nearly 50 years an excellent forum for experimental and traditional theatre, thanks to Micheál and Hilton, but whether they liked it or not the Longford company was there too and the legacy of the Gate must also include them.

It was during one of 'the boys' seasons as tenants of the Gate that Edward Longford and his wife Christine went on holiday to Greece. They saw a performance of *Oedipus* there which immediately struck them as being a perfect vehicle for Mac and as soon as they returned home they spoke to him about it.

Mac had thoughts of playing Oedipus but didn't particularly like Gilbert Murray's translation because it was rhymed, nor did he care for Yeats's version which he said was lacking theatrical punch, so he'd given up the idea of playing it. However, when Edward, a roly-poly 'boule de suif' of a man, jovial in a reserved, aristocratic sort of way suggested that he would do a translation especially for Mac whom he greatly admired, Mac was naturally delighted.

Eventually the finished translation was handed over to Mac and he started work on it and the usually agony of learning lines began once again. The good thing was that he wasn't under pressure to produce it by a certain date; he could take his time, and he did. After months of breaking it in, he felt comfortable enough to invite Edward and Christine down to the beautiful little Theatre Royal in Wexford, home for many years now of the well-known opera festival, (now replaced by a brand new opera house) for their first viewing of *Oedipus*.

That night in Wexford must have been something special to remember, though I confess I've no specific memories of it. I was 15 and in it from the beginning, playing the non-speaking part of one of Oedipus' two daughters who lead him when he's blind, the other was a local Wexford girl.

Christine Longford recalled what she saw:

> The curtain went up on the Palace at Thebes...I have never seen Mac look more marvellous. Why? Because he looked like himself for once, only taller than ever in his long robes, a tall beardless heroic king.

She goes on to describe the audience reaction when they first see him after he has blinded himself.

> There were screams in the audience, quite properly at the sight of that face covered in blood, but he hushed them with his beautiful voice ... as the curtain fell we were all sure that this terrible thing had happened, and why it had happened.

The Irish Times critic, who'd travelled from Dublin to see the play, reported:

> The performance recalled the spell with which we used to be held by great acting, one felt once more the tense hush, the utter stillness which only the finest playing can command.

The words of Gerry McLarnan, then a young actor in the company, spoken unrehearsed in the BBC tribute is for me the most affecting. He described Mac's agony when he's told by the shepherd that he has murdered his own father:

> Then he gets rid of the shepherd and he's got about three lines before he goes off, well, Mac said those lines then started to scream and God it was the most terrifying and tremendous thing I'd ever heard in my life! It wasn't just a man screaming. You felt this had come up really from the blasted pit. It came up through his feet, his legs, his genitals, his throat, his head, up and up and it wasn't one note only but a whole series of notes. It was absolutely terrifying and amazing.

Oedipus became one of Mac's great parts, remembered by all who saw it as extraordinary and it seems absurd and invalid for me to say anything even a trifle dissenting, but I felt my father was not completely secure as Oedipus. He was always very tense before playing it. But with his great Shakespearean parts one could see he loved and understood them according to his interpretation inside and out and within their contexts he was relaxed. With Oedipus it was an ordeal. The part was still new to him and he was fearful his memory would let him down. Mana must have felt this, but obviously the audience didn't or even the company; however, those were still the early days. By the early 1950s Mac was well under the skin of Oedipus when Harold Pinter was with us and he wrote in his essay:

> His concentration was always complete as Oedipus. He was at his best in the part. He acted with acute underness and tenacity and he never used his vocal powers to better or truer effect. He acted along the spine of the part and never deviated from it.

I trust my instincts though; my father's tenseness and nervousness was not imagined, and it was almost two years after the Wexford performance attended by the Longfords that he accepted their invitation to play it in Dublin.

19 – Fire, Lights, and the War

The company was on tour in the far reaches of Donegal and Mac was in Dublin playing in Emlyn Williams' *The Light of Heart* when we were devastated by a fire that burned down the hall in the town of Ardara and with it everything we owned. It couldn't have happened at a worse time, the third year of the war when most things were impossible to replace. 'The only thing that was salvaged,' as Mac liked to tell the nuns at convent matinees, was 'an elaborate brass crucifix' used in *The Cardinal*, 'heavily encrusted with precious jewels.' Actually, it wasn't the only thing. Happily two hampers of Shakespearean costumes were saved, stored in the garage at the cottage.

Losing so much was a very large blow. I think of the exquisite 18th century costumes and Daddy's treasured lighting equipment, the music, and the rich velvet tabs, the accumulation of 16 years of touring. Mana left at once for Dublin to beg, borrow, and buy anything she could. Mícheál and Hilton were wonderful and let her have whatever she needed and the Longfords did too. In the meantime, the company with only the clothes we stood up in (everyone's personal belongings were gone too) continued uninterrupted and we did a performance – if you could call it that – in the basement of the tiny Presbyterian Church. The play was *Love from a Stranger*, and we did it on a bare platform at one end of the room, the only lighting was from two bare bulbs hanging from the ceiling. The women borrowed each other's clothes and the men wore whatever they were wearing whether it was suitable or not. The little hall was jammed that night, it seemed everyone in the town turned out to support us, and they were probably a little curious too, to see how we'd do!

Replacing the costumes would be difficult but Mac, uncharacteristically resourceful in emergencies, thought of a 'scheme' to save the day. He thought of his friends, the clergy, and the rich fabrics used for vestments by the bishops and the priests and off he went to a leading ecclesiastical shop in Dublin and in an orgy of 'squandermania' bought whole bolts of brocades, satins, and rich velvets. He came away with the knowing look of someone who'd just pulled off a successful heist!

The costumes made of those materials turned out to be some of the most beautiful we'd ever had, but Mac wasn't satisfied, and off he went again to the same shop to buy more, but this time he was greeted by a hostile manager, who told him he couldn't have a yard more of anything. No new supplies were coming from Italy and what was the clergy to do?

The loss of the lights was the biggest blow to my father. For a touring company they were elaborate and sophisticated and they were his pride and joy. The actor, T.P. McKenna, in the BBC tribute commented on Mac's obsession:

> McMaster was one of the world's authorities on lighting, it fascinated him, which seemed contrary to his nature being as technical as it is. Over the years he learned everything he knew by doing. I'm quite sure he never studied a book on design of how to get a special effect.

But for all his serious interest in it, he couldn't resist being 'naughty' sometimes, experimenting with colour slides even during a performance! This was a paradox in his character, on one hand he went to great trouble and expense to get the right effect and then 'blew it' by doing something outrageous in full view of the audience! There are many wild stories of Mac's fascination with lights and some of the antics he got up to; some have become exaggerated over the years and some simply not true.

From *All for Hecuba* is Micheál's account of a performance of *The Merchant* when he was playing Lorenzo and is one of the best:

> ... as we sat (he and Jessica) in the garden together, ... Mac, who had received some new coloured mediums (gels) from London, began to play with the lighting. The glow on our faces changed suddenly from its pale and decorous blue to a most upsetting nuance of cyclamen, then to a blinding white, then to a vaporous green. A little shaken we continued; 'On such a

night stood Dido with a willow in her hand...' we were now bathed in a rosy sunset, followed by a dazzling lemon-coloured dawn and then came a sound of light footsteps and my sister Marjorie's agitated voice, 'Mac, Mac! Leave those lights alone, you are not to play with them during the show.' Complete blackout followed and then we were wafted once more into the public gaze in a glare of brilliant amber sunshine, which gave way at once to a sullen purple twilight. 'The man that hath no music in himself...' I struggled on. 'Mac, put those mediums down,' said Mana from the wings, 'are you mad? You've no conception of how it looks from the front.'

Mac was at least offstage when this episode happened (embellished by Micheál) but he was known, too, to change gels in the middle of a scene he was in. He was like a little boy with a new mechanical toy who had to see how it worked at once whether it was an appropriate time or not. The urge to see the effect of different coloured gels was stronger at the time than the interruption of the play or how it looked from the front. But Mana didn't let him get away with such naughtiness very often. I suppose each of us sees the characteristics in people through different eyes. She kept a close eye on him, sometimes quietly scolding him as if he were 10 years old.

I've said that my father was childlike, curious, how if you're an adult to be childish sounds derogatory but to be childlike is endearing. But, Harold Pinter wrote in his essay: 'Mac wasn't childlike as some have said. He was evasive, proud, affectionate, mischievous, merry, cynical, sad ...'

Mac may have been all the above and much more, we are all made up of many and sometimes contradictory components, and Mac *was* childlike. Mana knew it and talked to him quite often as if he needed things explained in as simple terms as possible. He had the spontaneous joy and the sudden despair of a child. His pranks with the lighting were hardly the behaviour of an adult! He would disappear if Mana needed to discuss something important that he didn't want to deal with. He was easily bored and to relieve it he went to endless films when he was between tours, just to fill in the day.

It's no wonder Mana had so little time left for Chris and me. Looking after Mac was a full-time job; keeping him in check, humouring him when he was, as Micheál once said, either 'Riding on the crest of his own enjoyment', or he was in the depths of despair and life was unmitigated hell!

It seems to me there are certain people who are put on this earth to express one unique talent. Extraordinary people, they have one passion, one reason for living, all else is unimportant (even if they might wish it were not so). They are exciting to know. They have a special aura about them, they are unpredictable, often maddening and they hardly know what's going on in the world around them. My father was one of these people, as I know everyone who ever knew him would agree.

It seemed curious, Mac's apparent detachment from the war. Politics never interested him and he hated violence so he removed himself from it, but what about the horror of the six million people Hitler slaughtered? Was Mac callously unaware of it all? To do him justice, no one in Ireland knew at the time that this was going on. The carnage in Dachau and Auschwitz was kept well hidden until the end of the war. When he did know, Mac spoke of all the genius that would never be known because so many of the world's greatest artists had been Jewish.

Christopher on the other hand kept up avidly with the war. He knew every strategy, defeat, and victory of the allies. He could have written a detailed account of it and he should have. My mother hardly talked about the war, probably because the memories of the First World War were still painful when she lost several of her friends and particularly her beau, Bay Morris.

Actors are well known for not being political (though that has changed in recent years) and I don't remember anyone in the company ever mentioning the war except that they had to get away from it. And it seemed very far away to me and except when Chris would insist on explaining the latest campaign of General Montgomery or General Eisenhower and he'd draw intricate maps and the position of their advancing troops, I hardly knew what was going on, but I was barely thirteen when the war began and like most girls – I like to think – it didn't much concern me, at least for a time.

I've wondered why I wasn't more inquiring at this time of my life. My shyness was an impediment. I hardly ever gave an opinion or asked questions and I was thought to be the 'not very bright' one of the family. This came about one day when my father, Chris, and I were walking in St. Stephen's Green in Dublin and Daddy came across an acquaintance. He greeted him with, 'Hello Squire', a salutation he used when he couldn't remember someone's name, and they talked pleasantries for a couple of minutes, then Mac remembered that we were there and introduced us. 'This is my son, Christopher,' he said with exaggerated paternal pride, 'a great blessing to us. And this is Mary-Rose', then turning away conspiratorially, he said in a stage whisper that made me all the more keen to hear: 'she's not very bright you know!'

He may not have meant it, said it for dramatic effect, or just because he thought it was amusing. In any case, the words stuck in my mind and I must have concluded that if I wasn't capable of learning, I simply wouldn't try!

20 – Facts of Life

The war dragged on and I was growing up but not without difficulties. The cough I'd had since the pneumonia in Scotland was insistent. I couldn't lie flat because mucus collected in my lungs and I had to sleep sitting propped up on pillows. Sometimes I coughed on stage, and when a few years later I played Desdemona to my father's Othello and the exertion of being strangled made me go into a paroxysm of coughing, Mac knew that it was agony to try to suppress it and was very accommodating. He would lift up his arms with his great robe spreading out like a sail on either side and out of the corner of his mouth he'd whisper, 'Cough, cough.' Then a little later when he said 'Let me the curtains draw.' I was out of view and the audience was at least spared from seeing a dead woman heave and choke but surely they must have still heard me!

I've wondered sometimes why I never saw a doctor or a dentist in my growing up years. I was reminded of the reason quite recently by a dear and very elderly friend, that in those days one didn't go near a doctor unless you were dying. Preventative medicine was hardly practiced then and anyway I was afraid of doctors. Something really serious might be discovered! And I did my best to hide my cough (and anything else that might be wrong) and fortunately my parents took no notice of it.

One day however, not long after the fire and Mana was still in Dublin with Mac gathering whatever they could to replace what was lost, a cyst on a bone burst and I arrived at the cottage with my face swollen beyond recognition. My mother said all I could do was point to my face as my tongue was so swollen I couldn't talk. I remember the terror I felt as I went to the doctor. He'll find out I have TB, or perhaps a tumour on the brain. He'll tell me I have only a few months to live!

In fact, the doctor sent me to a dentist who removed teeth from my upper jaw in order to operate on the cyst, but I've wondered since if it could have been done without losing my teeth? I was about fifteen at the time and naturally I didn't question the doctor's decision, what did I know? I didn't know anything about periods either and no one, least of all my mother, had ever discussed it with me. Then one evening my father took me to the opera and dressed me up in a beautiful lamé dress used in *The Cardinal* and not at all suitable for a girl of my age with no visible bosom! Halfway through *Madame Butterfly*, I felt a rush of something warm and sticky and I was horrified to find it was blood. My God, I was praying – am I to die so young? My inside is dropping out, dear Lord, let me get home to the cottage, and I did without my father knowing and I didn't tell Mana – hoping it would go away but it didn't – and the next day I sat with her on a cliff near the cottage and told her nervously that perhaps I'd eaten too many tomatoes! I'll always remember what she said, it seemed so Victorian and sweet if not very informative. She said: 'Women get these little arrangements once a month about your age, it's to let you know if you're having a baby or not.'

Yes, I was naïve, but then it was a different time (my two daughters knew about such things at the age of twelve or thereabouts). No one had talked about sex with me and I didn't inquire, but I knew it had something to do with being close to a man, how close I had no idea. The whole thing disgusted me and I avoided listening to sexual gossip that seemed to intrigue actors. My father loved it and a naughty twinkle would light up his bright blue eyes when describing someone's latest exploits. Outside the theatre the country people thought of sex as embarrassing and not to be talked about, so I remained in ignorant bliss for several more years.

Someone asked me once in the deadly game of Truth or Consequences if I knew the true relationship of Micheál and Hilton. Homosexuality was to me some vague thing of men liking their own sex and women too, but I had no idea of the physical ramifications and didn't want to know. I answered that Micheál and Hilton were professional partners and best friends and hoped to leave it at that, but I'd have to have been positively witless not to have known that Micheál was different from other men. What about the layers of makeup, the black mascara, and black toupee that I discovered many years later he'd no need of wearing at all. Once my father asked him why he didn't allow a few discreet strands of gray to be added when it was time for a new one. Micheál replied defiantly, that as long as there was a chemist shop nearby, that would never happen! Micheál never tried to conceal his gayness; indeed he enjoyed it and exploited it to the hilt. It never occurred to me however, that my father was bisexual! Even after I was grown and, I like to think, less naïve did it ever cross my mind.

I truly believe that sex wasn't very important to my father. His attitude toward it was like a boy who'd just discovered it and thinks of it as naughty, something to be whispered about with knowing looks.

However, since there has been some talk since his death here and there about Mac's bisexuality, I am compelled to try to set the matter straight, though nowadays it seems unnecessary as it's talked about openly, but when the talk, or in this case the printed word is actually libellous, I very much resent it and I need in memory of my father, to set the matter straight.

In Barbara Leaming's biography of Orson Welles, she writes about Orson's early days when he joined the Gate Theatre Company. She quotes Orson explaining how Micheál and Hilton met in Anew McMaster's legendary 'Intimate Shakespeare Company' (it was never called that). He 'was the *best* living Shakespearean actor. He was the most beautiful man you ever saw in your life – and with a marvellous voice. He had everything … (and) about McMaster's notorious reputation in England and Ireland, Orson laughed that '… he was a raging queen and went through the choir boys of each town like a withering flame!'

I'd like to know how my father could have toured the towns of Ireland large and small for nearly thirty-five years, returning over and over to the same towns where the clergy and the townspeople adored him, if he'd had such a reputation?

I doubt that Orson ever said such a thing. Given that he admired my father so enormously why would he have mocked him in this way? Simon Callow writes in his biography of Orson Welles that it was Anew McMaster who left an indelible impression on his (Welles) imagination. He saw him whenever he could. McMaster stayed in his mind as the embodiment of what an actor might be.

What Welles took back home (referring to his time at The Gate) [was] an experience of acting that stayed with him to the last. It was neither provided by Edwards, nor even by Mac Liammóir, whose romantic self-consciousness he admired but never sought to emulate. It was Anew McMaster who left an indefinable impression on his mind as the embodiment of what an actor should be ... and whenever he wrote of his ideal actor, it was McMaster he described, whether he knew it or not ...

Orson Welles wrote that the actor, T.P. McKenna, in the BBC tribute had such insight and put the matter into perspective when he said:

> Mac never grew up emotionally after the age of twelve and had all that childishness and glee. He was a very innocent man and his gayness as such I'd only heard about, I never saw it manifest itself in terms of attempt to seduce. He was a very A-sexual man.'

About Mac's relationship with my mother, whom he often called 'Mummy', T.P. McKenna went on to say:

> His homosexuality meant nothing, not compared to Marjorie, she was the be all and end all of his life, a really remarkable team. I would say that Mac was her child. She had two children; she had Christopher and she had Mary-Rose, but Mac was in a sense her only child.

21 – Burgess, Paulette and *Winterset*

It took several years before we completely recovered from the fire but we did and we went on touring and when someone asked me what part of Ireland I was from, I'd say, 'All of it', for there was hardly a town in the whole country I didn't know.

Chris and I became seasoned actors. The seven or eight Shakespeare plays we did constantly I knew like the back of my hand – and to the best of my understanding – and almost nothing about the rest of them.

Not continuing school was not a good thing for me. Yes, there are many who have gone on to live successful lives who have had little or no formal education – Micheál was one – but they are motivated and exceptional people. I was neither and like my father, if I didn't want to do something I didn't and no one made me.

However my life on the road gave me a deep love of the classics and especially Shakespeare and my love of opera was engendered by my father and I have loved it all my life.

I may have stumbled through life as a child but my convictions about things that interested me has always remained strong. My love of God has remained the most constant force in my life, my passion for animals and music has never changed and I love the theatre. The theatre that I knew, that is. I find it difficult to like much of what goes on in the theatre today, and my father would certainly have thought he'd died and gone to hell!

The inevitable and large changes in the past 40 years would have been too much for him to bear. Change can be difficult for anyone but for Mac, not entirely comfortable and in his own time the theatre today would be unrecognizable. 'Where is the magic?'

I can hear him saying, speaking of the physical changes. 'The lights are all exposed, there is no front of house curtain, and stage hands wander on in full view of the audience hauling off scenery and props. The mystery is all gone.'

I see his point to a degree. Obviously there's a place for theatre in the round and productions such as Mac might have described, but I also like the expectation of what's behind the front curtain. (The one place one can still count on that is opera.) I suppose I am behind the times too because I like to see a full set instead of the abstract pieces used nowadays, and I see little reason to transplant Shakespeare to the space-age or to one that is alien to the story and to the language.

It's as well our life span is only the length it is, we have to deal with so many horrendous changes. God is good. He knows when it's time to leave it all to the coming generations.

I've remarked before that touring would seem to be an unambitious way for my father to spend so much of his life, but he was always happiest on tour where he could be himself. He was well aware of the limitations of his nature, not his talent but his nature. Micheál wrote '... he was the most uneven of actors', which he regarded as one of Mac's greatest attributes because it allowed him the freedom to reach some of his most glorious moments onstage.

Harold Pinter spoke of Mac's unevenness in his essay:

> At his best, he was the best Othello I have ever seen, but he was capable of course of many indifferent and off-hand performances, on these occasions an edgy depression and fatigue hung over him ... at such times his eyes would fix upon the actors, appraising them coldly, emanating a grim dissatisfaction with himself and his company.

But it must be added that even on an 'off' night, as Harold said, 'He always gave his patrons their money's worth!'

His inspired performances were entirely unpredictable. They had nothing to do with where he was playing, if the house was jam-packed or if someone of importance was in front. In fact this could 'throw' him and he'd be 'off'. His off nights were usually the result of some quite small occurrence. Someone had said something tactless to him before he went on. He could be put off by a small house, or if the lightning was messed up. These things would take the edge off and he was not able to control it.

It's no wonder he loved the country audiences where the 'limitations of his nature' were not judged and where they also saw his greatest performances.

Carl Falb, in his dissertation, speaks of this:

> One may lament that McMaster's Oedipus was never seen outside Ireland ... This Oedipus was born in one of the country towns, and it was in the towns that it stayed ... his ego didn't require applause in London and New York – especially at the cost of his freedom. Those who saw McMaster are sad that none of his art was recorded on film or television tape ... (but) it is likely that even film could not have caught Mac's talent. The missing element would have been St. Johns Hall in Tralee, the Confraternity Hall in Thurles, the Ideal Cinema in Westport, The Boat House in Cappoquin, the local theatres of all kinds with the townspeople that made the essential contribution to the completion of Mac's art.'

We toured solidly until the end of the war and Mac didn't play in Dublin again until the end of 1946 when he joined Micheál and Hilton at the Gaiety Theatre in a production of *Trilby*. It turned out to be quite a family affair. Adapted by Micheál, what was wrong with the adaptation we'd used on tour? Micheál, always canny about money, probably had an eye on the royalties! Mac, naturally played Svengali, Christopher was Little Billie, and Cousin Sally was Trilby.

Mac was in his element, playing, as *The Irish Times* reported: .... 'as luscious a piece of melodrama as has been seen since the days of Tod Slaughter ... .' Yes it was pure melodrama; the kind of part Mac relished but didn't take too seriously. He romped through them, enjoying himself thoroughly, Fagin in *Oliver Twist* was another and so was Shylock, though a more contained version.

As Little Billie, the naïve young man in love with Trilby who becomes a victim of Svengali's wicked machinations, Chris had the quality of a little boy that had had a cruel trick played on him, bewildered, disappointed, crushed. Physically, Chris was all over the place. He didn't have Mac's grace, in fact, he was quite awkward. His feet when standing were usually at right angles to his body and his hands looked as if they were controlled by the strings of a marionette. His Fool in *Lear* was the best imaginable, innocent, sad, vulnerable but never self-pitying, and his physical awkwardness added to the pathos.

As an actress, Sally was the exact opposite of herself. She seemed self-conscious on the stage, lacking definition of character and rather affected in her movements. Off stage she was a free spirit, a true Bohemian. She lived exactly as she wanted and with whom she wanted and didn't care what people in Catholic Ireland in the 1940s thought. She looked Polynesian with brown almond shaped eyes, sallow skin, and dark curly hair and she dressed in hand painted cottons reminiscent of African women.

I admired her independence and her sense of freedom. She and I became good friends and correspondents later in life in spite of being quite different. I had a conventional side to my nature, wanting things to be orderly, probably because they never were. Sally thrived in a chaotic muddle! I loved the traditional rituals of the Catholic Church and Sally would sit cross-legged on a prayer mat and mutter mantras to African gods. Her background had been in London which explains her freedom of spirit. Her unconventional style of living was not unusual there, but not at all usual in Dublin at that time.

With the war over, travel between countries began again and with it an exhilarating feeling of liberation, for though Ireland was neutral and relatively unaffected by the war, there had been a sense of restriction that comes with being confined to an island.

Aunts Doff and Peg came flying over from England. After four years they were anxious to see brother Micheál and Little Marge as they called my mother. Mac, oddly, didn't seem to be in any hurry to spread his wings and after *Trilby* closed, he followed it at once with *She Stoops to Conquer* also done at the Gaiety. In the next year, as if to make up for the nearly four years he'd been out of Dublin, he did a total of ten plays there, most of them he was in, the rest he directed. He leased the Gate from Micheál and Hilton when they went on tour in the Balkans and at one point had two productions running in Dublin at the same time.

Perhaps the most noteworthy event at this time was the production of *Winterset* by Maxwell Anderson. Burgess Meredith and Paulette Goddard came from America to play the leads. Micheál played Troc, the Capone-like gangster and Mac was Judge Gaunt, an appropriate name since he became ill with jaundice during rehearsals, turned a pale shade of green, lost weight and remained in this condition for the run of the play.

The rest of the company was made up of actors from our company and the three leading Dublin theatres, each with distinctive ways of speaking English. The Abbey with their lovely authentic country accents, the Gate and their 'artsy' cultured Dublinese and the Olympia that spoke the Queen's English, both real and acquired as the Olympia did mostly light English comedies.

Ria Mooney, the distinguished actress and director of the Abbey, directed. *Winterset* was, of course, a huge financial success. Dubliners were eager to see real live film stars and Paulette was a big name at the time. The fact that she could not be heard beyond the first three rows didn't seem to matter a bit. The critics were kind to her and glowing in their praise for Burgess.

During the run, my parents invited Burgess and Paulette to the cottage for a picnic in the garden. Paulette looked cute with pigtails and a sunburned face (where did she get it from, surely not in Dublin?). She told Mana that she'd put her precious jewels in a safe in the Bank of Ireland. 'I realized right away, 'she said,' that I couldn't wear them here, it would look like I'm trying!'

Burgess was small and impish with a smile that weakened the knees. He'd have made a perfect Puck in *The Dream*. I'm sorry I barely remember his performance as Mio. Before he left Dublin he gave my father a framed photograph of himself and on it he wrote, '*Mac, McMaster, Magnificent.*' Sadly, like so much memorabilia, it vanished out of the house after my mother died.

22 – Pembroke Road and Some Actors

Soon after *Winterset* closed, Mac produced *Oliver Twist*, also at the Gaiety, mostly so that he could play the macabre and conniving Fagin. Micheál said he modelled his performance on Herbert Tree's Fagin and he probably did. It was another opportunity to go back in time to a past era of acting. One could see that he was having the time of his life.

I had been in heaven, home for almost a whole year, unheard of. It was the longest time I'd ever stayed in one place in my life so far. I mowed the grass, planted pretty flowers, did the house work (Mana hated it!) and looked after Bran, Deliah-Puss and Debussy Cat and I was gloriously happy. Daddy called me the 'drudge' because I was always cleaning something!

Then Jack came into my life. A little lost terrier I found one day in Dublin who sat down beside me as I waited to cross the street. I named him Jack but mostly I called him Backy-boy and we loved one another instantly. From then on I brought him on tour with me and he was the reason I didn't go with the family to Australia, but I'm jumping ahead.

The year in Dublin had been good for my father and especially for the company who had laid down some roots and made friends and had become part of the Dublin theatre scene. Several of our company stayed at number 3 Pembroke Road, a famous theatrical boarding house in the district of Ballsbridge. It has long since gone but in its time was well known to every visiting actor that ever came to Dublin. It was run by Mrs Lambert and later by her daughter, Mrs Ball. The Lamberts and the Balls were genteel Dublin Protestants. One could always tell a Protestant, there was a look about them. Cathleen Ball though could hardly be described as genteel. She was big and bouncy with what Aunt Doff would describe as 'an ample bosom' and she had the dirtiest laugh I'd ever heard! Everyone loved her, she had a huge heart and treated wayward and nomadic actors as if they were her special children.

The basement kitchen at the Lamberts was the focal point of the house where everyone gathered. The enormous well-scrubbed table was always laid for a sudden meal and how inviting it was. Pots of homemade jams and marmalade, mounds of fresh butter, homemade bread, and tea that seemed to be brewing all day long. Anyone who just casually dropped in was invited to stay for tea, high tea that is, rashers and eggs and sausage – of course – or cold ham and salad.

Amongst our actors to stay there over the years were Eugene Wellesley and Jack Aranson (who figured largely in my life because I married him!). Jack was fascinated with Eugene's stories of when he was with Sir John Martin Harvey, the famous English actor-manager and the three of us would stay up half the night in the comforting warmth of the huge iron range. Eugene in his element and Jack an intrigued listener. How many actors passed through this four-storey Georgian house is difficult to guess, but it must have been thousands, going back to the middle 1800s when Dublin was a number 1 touring date and was visited by the leading actors, dancers, and opera singers of the day. Number 3 flourished right up to the 1960s when, after Mrs Ball's death, her brother sold it.

Speaking of actors, so many came and eventually left our company in the 18 or so years I was with it, and most of them from the early days leading up to the 40s are vague to me now. Some went on to do well in London on the stage and in films. Pat Magee was one from the early years. He was from the north and had a wee Ulster accent which he tried to hide with his own version of a standard English one. An unhappy soul in his personal life, he seemed to be tortured by demons that only allowed him fleeting moments of peace. He was a gifted actor and I remember him especially as Iago. His performance was macabre, almost the stock villain, which in lesser hands might have been melodramatic, but it was him - his performance was completely real and truthful. In life, Pat had a dark side, sinister and complicated, which effortlessly transferred itself to Iago.

In the late 1950s he had a big success in the West End with his performance as Marat-Sade, a part that might have been written for him and he played in several British films, usually cast as the heavy. Sadly he died much too young at a time when his career was at its peak.

An endearing fixture in our company was of course Eugene. He'd known Chris and me since we were young children. He was always old to me, but he was probably no more than 50 when he first joined us. His sense of humour was English and disparaging but never cruel. He was a link with a past theatre, an 'actor-laddie' in the best sense, and everyone loved him.

This little story is typical of Eugene's reaction to a difficult moment on the stage. During a matinee of Priestley's play *An Inspector Calls* in Thurles Co. Tipperary, Harold (Pinter) who was in the cast, missed his cue to enter. Some minutes went by, probably moments which seemed like minutes and still the door did not open and no Harold came in. The actors on the stage began to make up dialogue to fill the awkward silence. One by one the four actors began making up quite believable lines but when it came to Eugene's turn, he just puffed a bit harder on his pipe, and turned to the actor who had spoken last and said, audibly, 'I'm damned if I'm going to ad-lib, old dear, go and fetch him. Find him! Find him – he's probably downstairs playing billiards!'

Eugene found humour in almost everything. Even in not being able to go! One day he was chuckling quietly to himself and chewing on his ever present pipe as he described how he'd had to walk half a mile (actors always exaggerate) down a path to the outhouse. 'By the time you get there the urge to go has worn off and there's no bum fodder (toilet paper) so you have to stay bunged up. It's all bloody hopeless!'

From the really early years, Esme Biddle stands out because of her beautiful speaking voice, her tall Romanesque figure and her 'secret' drinking, which everyone knew about because it affected her speech. When she'd drink taken – and sometimes she resorted to raw alcohol – she developed a lisp, so that the famous 'quality of mercy' speech in *The Merchant of Venice* came out: '... but merthy is above thith theptered thway ...' She looked gorgeous, elegant and regal in her red velvet lawyer's robe, though her make-up often looked as if she'd just come in from the rain. Esme travelled with her tiny sister who watched over her like a mother, once propping her against a lamppost while she went for help guiding her into the hall.

Shamus Locke was from the early times too. He was working as a postman in Navan Co. Meath and after seeing many of our plays, decided acting was what he really wanted to do and he asked my father if he could be a super in the crowd scenes in the Shakespeare plays. He was incredibly handsome and was then about 18 or 19 years old. Tall with a mass of beautiful black curly hair and eyes the colour of sapphires. By the end of the week in Navan he'd given up his job and became an apprentice in the company. Soon he was playing Rosencrantz, or was it Guildenstern? And one of the 'salads' (Salanino & Salarino) in *The Merchant*. Shamus eventually went to London and with his good looks and beautiful baritone voice he quickly became a star in musicals. Later in life and with his keen business sense he was successful in real estate and the stock market in the U.S. and with his wife retired to a splendid chateau-like house near San Diego. Oh, but 'what a falling off was there!'

Of course he was older when Jack and I visited him some years ago – we all were. After all, a gap of almost a lifetime had gone by since he'd been with Mac, and I would not have recognized him. How could Shamus have changed from the Adonis I remembered to this bald headed old man with false teeth that floated about in his mouth when he spoke?

But what was more alarming was his aura. He was bitter and critical of everything going on in the theatre of today. Now and again I would see a glimpse of the old Shamus when Jack, who loved theatrical history, would draw him out. Then Shamus would become animated and joyful and the old twinkle would light up his blue eyes as he spoke about touring with Mac and how it had been the happiest time of his life. Age was not sitting well on Shamus and I felt sad.

No wonder my father hated the idea of getting old, and it's worse for the beautiful people to see everything beginning to 'droop and drowse'. He would stand in front of a mirror sometimes pulling up his neck and his cheeks until his face looked stretched and expressionless. 'Oh Christ', he'd say, 'everything is going down, festoons of sagging flesh where you don't want it.'

Mac had a toupee he called his 'false piece' which he only wore on occasion at an interview (even if it was radio!) Or when he went to the opera or the opening of a play, and he didn't seem at all concerned that the fine mesh that glued it on to his forehead was clearly visible. I remember Micheál seeing Mac in the foyer of the Gaiety Theatre and saying in a voice designed to attract the intermission audience: 'Mac, you don't really expect people to believe that is actually growing on your head do you?' 'Not a word', Mac came back, 'not a word, the pot calling the kettle black and blacker it gets as the years creep up.' It's silly theatrical nonsense like this that I've missed for so many years, for it seems to me that if I moved in theatre circles now, which I don't, I would find that theatre people nowadays are not as theatrical and occasionally outrageous as they used to be!

Several more of our 'theatre people' were to become names after leaving us. In the early 50s came Harold Pinter and Kenneth Haigh, both just out of the Central School of Acting. A few years later, Kenneth scored a huge success in London as Jimmy Porter in the original production of *Look Back in Anger* by John Osborne. Harold became so well known as a playwright and actor that he needs no words of mine. Barry Foster was another who turns up regularly on British films and on TV, and T.P. McKenna, a lovely actor with a gentle cultivated Dublin accent, which for me is the best English spoken, has also done well in England.

The women in our company didn't fare as well. I mean that they didn't have the successes in England the men had, but this can be explained by the law of averages, since there are always more men in a classical theatre company than women. We usually had eight or nine men to three or four women.

One who stands out was Pauline Flanagan who joined our company in the early 50s. Later she did well in New York playing with the Irish Repertory Company and eventually returned to Ireland as a guest artist at the Abbey Theatre. She was young when she joined us, quite provincial and not all theatrical, a naïve convent educated girl from Sligo. Soon she showed a natural talent that only needed to be backed up by technique and experience, and she learned both with us very quickly, playing every kind of part! She had a classic maturity about her that made her seem older than she was, and in quite a short time she was playing parts like Jocasta in *Oedipus* and the Queen in *Hamlet*. I remember her Lady Macbeth especially. On the surface she was composed and in control, but inside a smouldering hell was brewing. One could feel it in the way she moved, a little restless like a caged animal. She looked marvellous, raven hair, shining eyes, and a kind of pallor to her skin that made her seem menacing. Off stage she was still the soft spoken unsophisticated girl from Sligo!

Pauline and Harold fell in love on tour and became inseparable. Both were beautiful and young and it looked like true love, but eventually they parted. They both married different people, but I believe they remained friends all their lives.

Most of the actors who passed through our company I think of with nostalgic affection. The theatre seems to attract eccentric, witty, even bizarre characters, and we had our share. But as their names are not known – except in their own circles – or they have gone now to a better place, I'll mention only two. One who became my very first boyfriend and the other because he surely was bizarre.

His name was Billy Quin, a country lad from Dungarvan. It was rumoured that he was gay, he was certainly outrageous and he loved it. This at a time when such 'quirks of nature' were not spoken of or admitted to. The most anyone in the country would say was 'God love him, he's a bit girlish, isn't he!'

Joining the company was freedom for Billy to behave and look as he pleased. He played Osric in *Hamlet* and Roderigo in *Othello*. For Osric he dyed his hair several shades of blond and his make-up and gestures put one in mind of Prince Albrecht in *Swan Lake*! What was bizarre was that at home in Dungarvan I believe he had a wife and four or five children!

Barry Keegan was a Dubliner, whom Mac invited to the company because of his passing resemblance to him, to play amongst other parts, his look-alike in *A Tale of Two Cities*. He was tall and blond with blue eyes, but there the resemblance ended, but it was enough. He was a good juvenile leading man type and I immediately had a crush on him! I was about 19 at the time, but still so young. He made me feel I existed by making a point of talking to me after rehearsal or a simple thing like saying 'wait, I'll walk up the street with you.' I couldn't believe he could actually be attracted to me! We never had an affair. I was much too green and had definite convictions that one didn't do that sort of thing unless you were married.

After several months of walking hand in hand – I quickly withdrew my hand if we came across another member of the company – Barry went to my father and formally 'asked for my hand'! 'Mac, would you ever let me marry your daughter?' he asked dramatically in his distinct Dublinese. Mac told him it was nothing to do with him and to ask me. I like to think it was Mac's way of avoiding giving an answer, because he didn't think it was a good thing. Barry remains significant because he was my first love.

23 – Australia Again

The company had been going now for 20 years and Mac was still as much in love with acting as ever. It was quite simply what he lived to do.

He did become bored though with interviewing new actors and re-rehearsing plays that had been in the rep. forever. Sometimes he hired an actor sight unseen or on someone's recommendation, gave him a week or so to study and rehearse 9 or 10 plays and he'd just hope for the best! This obviously was not fair to the actor or Mac and if the results were not good, Mac had only himself to blame.

By this time, I was playing most of the 'young things' parts like Mabel Chiltern in *An Ideal Husband,* Constance Neville in *She Stoops To Conquer* and whatever was needed in the 'frightful' plays. My favourites though were Ophelia in *Hamlet,* Celia in *As You Like It*, and Nerissa in *The Merchant*, and eventually Desdemona in *Othello*. Parts I thought of as mine own. How dare anyone else play them! At the time I especially loved Ophelia and at the risk of blowing my own trumpet, Siobhán McKenna, the eminent Irish actress said I was the best Ophelia she'd ever seen! I believe I was good in it and maybe that's why I loved it as I did, and it was my very own!

It was about this time however, I had one of my periodic rebellions against touring. I longed to be at home for a while; my mother agreed and enrolled me in Miss Galway's Secretarial School in Dublin, to give me a skill that could be useful when I returned to the company. So off I went to Howth with my little dog, Backy-boy who had travelled with me ever since I found him. I learned shorthand and typing fairly easily, but as I didn't know anything about arithmetic, (and still don't!) I had to drop book-keeping.

On tour in the meantime my very own parts were being played by Kitty Fitzgerald, a very proper young woman from Cork. I suppose I had a slight resentment for her, being a bit of a dog in the manger. I couldn't play these parts at the time, but I didn't want her to play them either! Kitty seemed to be disapproving of the theatre and theatre people. It was odd to me that she chose the 'sinful' life of the theatre as her profession. She was perfect in parts like St. Bernadette in a version of Franz Werfel's *Song of Bernadette* and Bella in *Gaslight* which she played opposite the menacing Pat Magee as her conniving husband. I remember how chilling she was when she's trying hysterically to convince him she's not losing her mind after he's been telling her for months that she is. She was unbelievably pitiful, heart breaking. I've never forgotten it.

When Backy-boy and I eventually rejoined the company, it was awkward, I could hardly wrench my special parts away from Kitty so it was decided, by Mana I think, that we should share them. A good solution, except it caused a bit of friction when we both wanted to play a certain part on the same evening. Friction that took the form of a slight hostility between us, but we didn't fight. I was too timid and she was too much the polite Victorian lady, but it was there. Fortunately, this awkward situation was resolved when Mac walked into rehearsal one morning and announced that the present tour was ending because we were going to Australia, 'Pack your bags dears,' he said, 'We're off to the Antipodes.'

It was late 1948 and Mac and Mana had been negotiating for the possibility of a season in Melbourne for some time, but had been silent in case it fell through. Now the contract was signed and they happily let the company know.

By mutual agreement a few of our actors stayed in Ireland or went back to England. Mac went to London and engaged several strong experienced people. The arrangements happened very quickly, everyone was hastily packing and getting passports, a wonderful adventure was about to begin and everyone was excited. Everyone except me. I didn't want to leave the cottage, the dogs and cats, and especially Backy-boy, so I refused to go!

Very soon, my family and the company were on their way to the Antipodes (which Mac pronounced as in explodes!) leaving with much fanfare on a P&O liner from Southampton. Mac however dreaded long sea voyages. He wasn't acting so it bored him, and he flew to Cairo and joined the ship at Port Said cutting the journey by about a week. It took five weeks in all after making calls at ports with names that made one think of *Kubla Khan* and the *Arabian Nights*.

Did I not feel even the slightest pang of regret that I was missing a wonderful experience? Not at all, all I wanted was to be at home and I was gloriously content.

I needed to work though, since at 22 I could hardly expect my parents to support me and so I asked Uncle Micheál if I could join them. 'Of course you can, you dreary cow' he said affectionately, and I did. It was the first time I'd be acting with a company other than my father's. I was beginning my own adventure.

I was paid £4.10 a week. £6.10 when we went to Scotland. Sounds so meagre, but it was quite usual for the time. In Glasgow, I almost expired from the effects of the dense khaki coloured smog that hung over the city and I was sent to stay in Ayrshire where the air was fairly clear. Micheál was always loving and kind to Sally and me. He seemed to take a paternal (or maternal?) interest in us. Once he looked at me and said 'You're not really going through the winter in that excuse for an overcoat are you?' And he took me out and bought me a new one! With Sally it was usually being sympathetic and supportive after her latest inamorata had let her down.

In Micheál and Hilton's company I shared the ingénue parts with Helena Hughes, a delicate English beauty, whose waif like quality belied her business sense and ambition. Micheál called her 'little bitch girl' – rather unkindly I thought – but he was wary of anyone who might get the better of him and he knew she could be wily.

Helena married a young actor in their company called Liam Gannon and a few years later they almost caused a disaster on Broadway when both were playing leading parts in Micheál's play *Where Stars Walk*. On opening night neither Liam nor Helena could be found! Panic! The stage manager and Hilton rushed to their hotel, expecting perhaps to find them passed out from altitude sickness (their rooms were on the 38th floor!) or some other emergency. Instead, they found them napping happily, ensconced in connubial bliss. Hilton was outraged. He strutted and bellowed and screamed and yelled. Unheard of before, the play began 30 minutes late – on Broadway!

Being with the Gate Theatre Company was very different from our company. Rehearsals went on sometimes to the early hours of the morning (obviously before unions). Hilton was a perfectionist and wanted every detail as he envisioned it, no compromises, and the actors, especially Micheál would become tense and argumentative. Hilton was the autocrat, absolutely, he conducted rehearsals with a heavy Germanic hand, no room for a trivial remark and if you missed a cue, God help you!

We did a play called *To Live In Peace,* first done at the Gaiety in Dublin and then in Glasgow, and I had volunteered to look after a flock of geese who were obviously frightened by the bright lights on the stage, and they were fluttering and struggling to get out of their cages. I felt sorry for them and one day, it was the dress rehearsal, I opened one of the cages to talk to them, when out fled two or three – wildly flapping their wings in panic. They flew onto the stage and then out into the auditorium, making that haunting sound of geese as they flew. Hilton was not amused 'What the bloody hell is she doing!', he yelled. I cowered somewhere behind a flat, too terrified to breathe. Hilton was fond of intimidating the younger members of the company and I was a perfect subject. I never dared to stand up to him or answer back but, as seems to be true with bullies, Hilton quickly retreated if anyone did. Apart from feeling terrified much of the time, I enjoyed this period with the Gate Company. I grew up a bit, became more independent. I played some good parts and made new friends.

Meantime, in far off Australia, the McMaster Company was making a very good impression. They had opened at the Princess Theatre in Melbourne and done *Othello, The Taming of the Shrew, Trilby,* and *Dr. Angles,* a play by James Bridie. The houses were packed and the audiences, mostly made up of Melbourne's elite, came in full evening dress. When the season ended, the company went on tour with the same repertory to Brisbane, Adelaide, and Perth in Western Australia.

Mac (Mana) remarked in *The Irish Times* articles how much Australia had changed in the 25 years since he'd been there. Before, he'd thought of 'Australian cities as rather tasteless second rate copies of London, but now Melbourne was a smart flourishing city with shops full of expensive and attractive things – lovely clothes, costly antiques ...'

They had been away over a year and, after the run in Perth, the English contingent, fearing, I suppose, that they may be missing opportunities in London, sailed for home. My parents and what was left of the company including Chris spent the winter languishing on the beaches near Perth. It was Christmas, the height of the Australian summer and Mac recalled eating roast turkey and plum pudding in weather of 105 degrees.

The season in Melbourne and the tour had taken them through the whole of 1949 and some of 1950, and Mac was ready to head for home. Then out of the blue, an invitation came from the Council of Adult Education in Melbourne, inviting the company to do a tour of Victoria. Why not? More adventure and off Mac flew back to Melbourne to recruit some Australian actors.

Meanwhile, in Dublin, I had fallen in love with a handsome student at Trinity College, full of charm and poetry. He swept me into an enchanted never-never land where only happy times exist. We had no passionate affair, I was still too Catholic and fearful. We spent a heavenly summer together and then suddenly he was gone.

Running away was all I could think to do. My heart was shattered, and I wired my parents that I was leaving for Australia as soon as I could. So I left the Gate and Howth, my darling dogs and cats, and took my constant companion, Backy-boy to England where I left him with Aunt Doff, promising to retrieve him on the way home.

In Southampton, I boarded the P&O liner The Strathnaver which didn't inspire me at all! Four weeks on a ship was not my idea of fun or a rest (I couldn't imagine people actually going on a cruise for pleasure!), but landing in Port Said was fun with the vendors scrambling to sell watches and radios that never worked and the bright colours and musky smell of the bazaars. We went through the Suez Canal, where there were snipers with rifles hiding in the dunes and we were instructed to go to our cabins or lie face down on the decks. I spent a lovely two days in Ceylon (now Sri Lanka) with my cousin Moira who had married a tea planter and lived in a mansion on a huge plantation. She had become a typical British Colonial wife and called her driver 'boy'. 'Does he not have a name?' I asked innocently. 'Oh yes,' she replied brightly, 'but you know I've never asked him what it is.

He is 'our boy'. No wonder the English lost their colonies! Moira was kind though and pretty. She was, I suppose, a product of her rather grand up-bringing.

At last, I arrived in Perth. A strange isolated city, like Las Vegas it rises unexpectedly and unnaturally out of the sand, with nothing near it in either direction but desert on the east and the Indian Ocean on the west. The early settlers, who were mostly convicts, called Perth 'the city of sand, sin, and sorrow,' and they had no chance of escaping.

My mother and the remaining company had already gone to Melbourne to begin rehearsals for the new tour and I stayed a few days with Chris who was working as a journalist on a daily newspaper and had decided to stay in Perth. He'd made some new friends who invited us to sumptuous barbecues on the beach where we ate enormous crayfish and prawns the size of bananas.

I soon realized that everything in Australia was enormous. The distances between places, the towering eucalyptus trees, the extravagance of their entertaining, and the people who all seemed to be at least a foot taller than anyone at home.

Chris loved it. Somehow, he'd been a square peg in a round hole for so long, but now he'd found his niche, he was writing articles about things that most interested him. History, changing political boundaries, conflicts in religion and the arts. I'd never seen my dearest brother so content.

After a week or so, it was time for me to join the company in Melbourne and I boarded the trans-continental train that would cross the vast Nullarbor Plain. 3,000 miles of flat arid land, no trees, no rivers, only scrub bush that had no leaves. About every 500 miles, a water tower would appear rising up out of this no-man's land like a mirage, and where we stopped to fill the engine with water. I wondered how the water got there. I suppose a train with nothing but huge tanks of water must travel on these never ending tracks when the passenger train didn't! I got out and wandered about during those stops together with other passengers. By turning in a circle one could see the entire circumference of the earth – it must be like walking on the moon! In a few places a small band of aborigines would shyly appear from where? Nowhere to hide, they were just suddenly there. Strange neolithic-looking people, who lived on witchetty grubs – worm like creatures that somehow survive in the scrub bushes. I wondered how these people could exist in this parched, treeless, and waterless place. It was astonishing. We stopped briefly in Adelaide and then on to Melbourne.

Rehearsals were in full swing when I arrived except that they had to be conducted with no Desdemona, Ophelia, and Bianca. Mac was relieved and happy to see me. 'The rehearsals have been patchy dear, very patchy. Walter has been reading Desdemona's lines and apart from being the wrong gender; those hands, and those feet...' You were supposed to know what he meant, and I did.

Any comparison between touring Ireland and touring Australia would be like comparing the Antarctic and the Hawaiian islands. The distances between towns was enormous, 200 and 300 miles apart. The company and the equipment travelled in a huge converted refrigeration truck, known as 'the monster!' The front end, high up over the driver's cabin had been converted into a bus with large plate glass windows and seated most of the actors. It was fairly comfortable but so hot! The air shimmers with heat and what strange country we saw. Still, uninhabited, timeless. Nothing but enormous eucalyptus trees peeling their bark in giant festoons.

Occasionally, a kangaroo or a wallaby would hop out of the bush, just curious to see who we were. Then suddenly out of the silence came the screech of a large (of course) bird called the kookaburra – a wild unearthly cry. I felt that we were travelling on virgin territory, uninhabited, unexplored, that we were the first humans ever to tread foot there.

Nonsense, because unexpectedly a little town would suddenly appear, plunked down in the middle of nowhere, 'Complete,' my mother wrote, 'with a swimming pool, a public library, and a large well equipped theatre – out of all proportion to the size of the town', built I suppose with the idea that the population would expand in the future. By now, I'm sure it has. Victoria was dotted with these oddly suburban self-contained little towns, so remote, so isolated. We played only two days in each town and off we went to the next. We seemed to live in 'the monster'!

After the play, our company was always invited by the ladies committee to what they called 'a bun fight', a casual reception with little sandwiches and tea. The mayor or school teacher made speeches about how privileged they were to have Anew McMaster and his distinguished company visit their town, but in one town the speaker called him Andrew Mac Alister! A glazed look came over my father's eyes as he tuned everyone out and he let the smoke from his cigarette linger about his head. He was no longer in Wangaratta – or wherever it was. Mac was never sure where he was. Didn't matter, he said, because all the towns look alike, the same faces of the ladies committee seemed to show up in every town, but once he thanked the kind people of Tangerma when we were actually in Yarrawonga!

The people were genuinely kind; they couldn't do enough for us. It was quite an event for them to have a theatre company visit all the way from Ireland. We played *The Taming of the Shrew*, *She Stoops to Conquer* and *Love From a Stranger*. Three plays that had nothing to do with their culture or their lives, but most of the citizens turned out in each town we went to.

By this time, I was happily getting over my lost Trinity student and I promptly fell in love again! He was an Australian actor in the company called Allan. We had a sweet and innocent liaison, but again, no affair. Which was just as well as I later realized that for me anyway, sex has a way of binding one to another and it's more devastating when it ends. At the time though, I was still afraid of sex, also just as well as Allan had a wife in Melbourne whom he said he was staying with for the sake of their little girl.

Almost immediately after the tour ended, another began, this time in Southern Australia, but Mac was getting restless. After visiting over 40 towns in Victoria, New South Wales and Southern Australia the wonder of the outback was wearing thin. Fearing another tour might be in the offing, my parents rushed to the nearest travel office to make arrangements before being tempted, but first Mac had in mind to do a short tour of India on the way home. It would be an interesting experience and he discussed the possibility with Walter. They knew there was an audience for Shakespeare. The English actor Geoffrey Kendall had been touring India for years. Mac reasoned that there could be room for new blood. So Walter was dispatched to India to make preliminary arrangements. Allan and I went to the ship to see him off. Dear old Walter, red-faced and good-humoured, we had no idea as we waved to him from the pier that we'd never see him again. After several weeks, Walter wrote to Mac from New Delhi that he'd secured the first few months of the tour and he felt that there was definite interest in our touring there. Then – without warning – he died suddenly, and the tour was abruptly cancelled.

Walter's death was a huge blow to my parents. He was first an old friend, and had been with the company from the beginning. He'd been a solid, steadying influence, especially when Mac was in one of his depressed conditions and wouldn't get out of bed.

My parents and what was left of the European members of the company sailed for home. One or two decided to stay on in Australia, and one or two Australians decided to go to Ireland with them. I stayed on in Melbourne because I'd not been in Australia as long as the others and I wanted to see more of it, but mostly I stayed because of Allan. I worked for a while in an expensive department shop called Georges, being too shy to go after any theatre work there might have been, but I was content. I was not ambitious (a curiously lacking trait in my family) and Allan and I saw each other every day – for a while – then one day he told me he was going back to his wife as his little girl needed him and that was the end of Allan. Oh dear, I'd done it again, a broken heart again and a need to run away again and I did!

Thousands of miles away in Perth, Christopher was going through his own crisis and a far more serious one than mine. He had swallowed dozens of aspirin in an attempt to kill himself!

Colm O'Doherty, a good friend of Chris, who had come with us originally from Ireland, and had married and settled permanently in Perth, wired me to come as soon as possible. I left at once. My own troubles faded as I raced once more across the Nullarbor Plain, this time by air. When I arrived Chris had been taken to hospital, his stomach pumped, and he was out of danger.

Poor darling Chris, what had gone wrong? His job, I thought, was satisfying, he'd fitted in well to the social life of Perth, and he'd seemed so happy. But Chris was isolated, lonely inside. It was difficult for him to really connect with people intimately. He craved closeness and affection, but was uncomfortable giving it and receiving it. It's difficult to know how much of this was his own nature and how much he was affected by the circumstances of his early childhood.

We both had weathered the myriad of changes in locale as children, the different faces of the people in charge of us and the uncertainties of where we'd land next, and we both had a different way of dealing with it. Chris insulated himself by building a fortress around himself and perhaps my going through my early years in a kind of limbo, not thinking much, not learning much, was my way of not having to deal with the absence of closeness we both felt from our parents. There is no blame. My father was a very unusual man, one with a unique gift, and he needed my mother's complete attention. Chris and I were, in a way, casualties of their extraordinary union.

    I accepted the status quo but Chris wanted so much more. His breakdown in Perth was, I believe, the result of years of suppressing his needs and the realization that, though he wanted now to tear down the walls he'd built around himself, he didn't know how.

    I stayed in Perth for about a year, keeping a watchful eye on my brother and working with the Australian Broadcasting Commission. Chris recovered, but he always remained psychologically fragile.

24 – Changing Times and Equity

I'd been in Australia almost two years and I had seen the Great Barrier Reef, Sydney for a few days, and the capital, Canberra, but it was time to go home. I longed for our cottage overlooking Dublin Bay and Backy-boy, Bran, Rover and the cats.

Change has always been difficult for me and I'd taken for granted that our tours would last forever, but when I returned there were signs of change for the company, and for me.

Touring Ireland had never been a money maker, even with generally full houses, but now with running expenses ever on the rise, and the competition of television, it's a wonder the company kept going at all. Even the little fit-up companies were going off the road one by one, but keep going we did. 'It was a remarkable effort' wrote Carl Falb in his thesis, 'The touring tradition was finished everywhere else.' But how long could we continue? For Mac, it was unthinkable that it should end, but so does life, and until that happens, he was determined to keep going.

For me, the change was personal and devastating. Soon after my parents had come home from Australia, they had given up the cottage. Couldn't Mana have warned me? It was the right thing to do from their point of view. Almost three years away had taken a heavy toll on my darling home. It was damp and decaying. Somewhere more accessible and convenient was needed and my parents had leased a flat at the back of Fitzwilliam Square in Dublin. It had all the amenities my adored cottage didn't but it had meant everything to me and the loss of it tore my tenuous security to shreds. I longed for it and now it was gone.

It didn't occur to me at the time that I was grown up now and it was time I moved away from the family nest, but ours was such a special nest! And, you might wonder, what about the cats and dogs? Bran and Rover (another dog I somehow acquired) who'd been living with Molly (our dear maid) and her family, simply stayed there, so did Delilah-Puss and Debussy-Cat. Aunt Doff who had had my Backy-boy since I'd left for Australia convinced me to leave him with her. 'He's old and it's not fair to uproot him,' she said. So here I was home without a home, without my dogs and cats, and still a little tender from a broken heart. I don't remember saying much about it to my parents. They were having troubles of their own.

A new obstacle was threatening the life of the company as Mac saw it, in the form of Actors Equity, the actors union, already a strong force in England and the cause of the demise of many struggling repertory companies there, and it had recently come to Ireland.

Mac resented the whole idea of unionizing the theatre and, from his position, rightly so. He had given employment to actors on a continuing basis for 25 years and it had only been possible because he and my mother had long experience and the ingenuity of how it could be done. They had brought excitement and drama into the lives of generally poor people who otherwise would never have been exposed to Shakespeare and the rest, and they had done it without private backing or subsidy. Now Equity wanted to dictate what salaries should be and impose impractical rules such as actors can *only* act, no assisting with the set-up, lights, or costumes, etc., which before they had agreed to and were quite willing to do.

For almost a year, Actors Equity was kept at bay by ignoring their letters and threats. Eventually Mana wrote them a letter asking them if they really wanted to be responsible for putting the company out of business as well as putting twelve or more people out of work? But in the end it was impossible to ignore. Equity had come to stay and we had to deal with it. A few concessions were made and Mac and Mana signed an Equity contract.

One of the actors, Gerry McLarnan was appointed Equity deputy – 'The Spy' as Mac called him. His job was to see that rules were not broken and if anyone had a grievance they should go to him. Gerry, who had been a valued and long-standing member of the company suddenly became the enemy in Mac's black-and-white way of looking at things. 'I've turned against him', he said with mock petulance, but Mac felt betrayed and he began to distance himself from the company. He was management, the enemy of the people.

For a time, Equity divided the company into pro-management and anti-management and damaged the time honoured relationship an actor had with the actor/manager which was special. He was a father figure to the younger actors. Watching out for them, advising and teaching them. Mac was such, though perhaps unconsciously. Just by being who he was, he was doing it, and the actors in turn truly loved him and admired him. Actors Equity unknowingly impaired this.

In fairness to Dermot Doolin, the General Secretary of Irish Equity, he wasn't quite the ogre that my father decided he was. It was his job to see that the rules set by English Equity were carried out, but things would never be the same.

1952. This was the year Harold, Barry, and Kenneth joined us. Ambitious, talented young men just out of the Royal Academy of Dramatic Arts, and The Central School of Acting in London, who needed experience. Also joining us at the time was Jack Aranson. I'll always remember the first day I saw Jack. I'd been home just a few weeks from Australia and staying with my parents in Fitzwilliam Square when one early afternoon and still in my pyjamas and dressing gown (not sure why!) I wandered into the living room where Mac was interviewing a dark, attractive young man who looked straight at me. It was Jack. I apologized for my appearance and slunk quietly into the kitchen. That was all, but years later Jack liked to say that he knew in those few seconds that he and I would be married one day!

Mac liked him and gave him a job and so did Mana, who admired people who weren't bound by possessions and Jack had everything he owned in a knapsack slung on his back. His clothes were unconventional for the Dublin of the day. He was a bohemian, as I found out later, in life style as well as in dress. His hair was black and curly and he wore bright green corduroy trousers, a scarlet bandana around his neck and a navy pea-jacket. He looked like Turiddu in *Cavalleria Rusticana*.

Mana flirted with him in her gentle Victorian way, but that changed when Jack showed an interest in me. Then she began to find fault in him. 'He doesn't speak good English,' she said, 'He mispronounces Shakespeare.' A bit harsh, but occasionally he did and I'd correct a word or two. Ironic, because 15 years later he delighted in correcting me!

An American from California, his accent was 'mid-Atlantic' as he liked to say. Two years at the Old Vic School in London, and before that studying the classics at the University of California had neutralized it, but his background was truly American. His father, an immigrant from Russia, was Jewish, his mother was Scottish, Irish and English, and an Episcopalian. If it were not for the theatre, the chances of our ever meeting were extremely improbable – or that we would spend the next twenty years of our lives together, after several dramatic partings and re-unions, also seemed unlikely – but we did.

My memories of this period, the actors in the company – until I left the company to spend so much of my life in America – are still quite vivid. Eugene was there, of course, how could we tour without him? Laurel Streeter, from Australia, who'd been with the company there and had come to Ireland with the assurance that Mac would give her work. A dark, striking woman in her 40s with a tongue on her that would make cowboys in a bar room blush, and there was Max Ettlinger, another graduate of RADA in London. Tall and good looking he was immediately enamoured of Sarah Malcolm, a pretty and sophisticated young actress who I remember especially as a lovely Rosalind in *As You Like It,* Pauline Flanagan and Penelope Parry, an actress from Canada who flirted with Jack, and the aforementioned contingent from England, Pinter, Haigh, and Foster.

These were the glamorous ones as I thought of them, but it was the Irish actors who were the bulwark, the solid foundation of the company who were there for years and who could forget Paddy Gardiner? – electrician and actor until Equity dictated he could be one or the other but not both. Paddy would have gone to the ends of the earth for my father. How many times was he up a ladder re-focusing a light or changing a gel at Mac's sudden request, when his cue to enter as Rosencrantz or one of the 'salads' was imminent. Poor Paddy, he was in a continuous state of confusion. There was Maurice Good from Dublin, tall, young, and handsome. Later he did well at the Old Vic Theatre in London. Joe Nolan also a Dubliner, eccentric, theatrical, comical, and a devout Catholic, he once played Tubal the Jew in *The Merchant of Venice,* with a large wooden rosary beads dangling from his belt!

From Dublin too, was Grania O'Shannon tiny, blonde, and dynamic. Her name popped up on the technical credits of many British films in later years. She was one of the remaining few who kept in contact from time to time. I was saddened to hear of her sudden death in December, 2010.

One who has quite recently left us is John Riggs-Miller, a gentleman farmer's son from Tipperary. He was young, about 24, when he joined the company and so good-looking and completely charming. He was smitten with the lure and adventure of being part of a travelling theatre company, and I was quite smitten with him, but he needed someone to take charge and make decisions for him. We'd have been a hapless pair! John was the opposite to Jack in almost everything. Jack loved to be in charge, and since I was shy and wanting in self-confidence, I thought he was what I needed.

My mind goes back to one of the last productions of *The Merchant of Venice* I was in, in Ireland. Pauline Flanagan was an imperious and charming Portia. I was Nerissa which I loved and I was playing opposite Jack as an ingratiating Gratiano. I can still see him so well, so graceful in his movements, balletic almost, smiling, and with a touch of wickedness. I can see him in his black tights and the burgundy-coloured velvet tunic trimmed with gold braid. A few years ago, I gave him the tunic; a reminder of another time when we were young, life was ahead of us, and we were together.

The Merchant was a night off for Mac and the cast. It was thought of as an easy play and we all enjoyed it. It was also the one Shakespearean play in which Mac allowed himself to be 'naughty'. One evening, in the famous court scene, Bassanio, played by Harold had the line 'For thy three thousand ducats, here are six', but Harold said 'buckets' by mistake and Mac answered quite seriously, 'If every bucket in six thousand buckets were in six parts and every part a bucket, I would not draw them I would have my bond.' Well, as Barry Foster recalled in the BBC tribute: 'Everyone in the court scene turned upstage to hide their faces, except Antonio and Bassanio who couldn't. Then Harold trying hard to stifle his humour grabbed his nose as one about to jump into the sea. Some of the others sauntered off stage.' Naughtiness aside, Mac was a great Shylock, the best I've ever seen. Many years later, Jack played Shylock and wore all Mac's costumes.

The differences between Jack and me were large and we were aware of it from the beginning. He was 27 and had 'been around', three years in the U.S. Navy, and his student days in California, where he'd sowed bushels of wild oats, as well as in London, where he'd had liaisons with more than one well-known married actress. He was a rogue, and it was one of the things that attracted me to him. My life on the road in Ireland, had been unconventional but – and perhaps it was because we were in Ireland – I was still naïve. Jack, with his colourful past and his exploits, represented something new and exciting and I was very flattered that he was attracted to me, but it was difficult for me to believe at first. I imagined he had an ulterior motive. Perhaps he wanted an 'in' with my father to be assured of work, or perhaps he had his sights set on parts like Iago or even Hamlet if Mac was absent, and he was using me to get them?! Why should he, this crazy attractive American, want me?

Eugene and Jack became fast friends. Gene of the old school and his stories of Martin Harvey, his mentor and his connection – if only by the era he lived in as a young man – to Henry Irving, Ellen Terry, Sir Frank Benson, and Mrs Patrick Campbell. I can see the pair of them walking in the country together. Gene animated, gesturing dramatically as he retold stories of the old days. Jack loved it, eagerly gobbling it all up and asking for more, more, more. In his own way, Jack, like my father, was attuned to the theatre of the past and his own productions later on were conservative and quite conventional. Jack stayed friends with Eugene until the end of his life and afterwards he kept in touch with his widow, Muriel, and later still with their daughter, Jane.

The tours continued and I remember it as a happy time. Christopher came back from Australia and rejoined the company and I was very glad to see him. The 'glamorous' English actors were a talented and interesting bunch who had a good humoured and quizzical attitude about the physical difficulties of touring Ireland. Harold was an observer, wryly commenting on the lack of comfort in the halls, the digs, the landladies, and the food.

Early in 1953, Mac was approached by a committee headed by Jack Dowling, a captain in the army, to play St. Patrick in a massive three day pageant. It was to begin with the arrival of St. Patrick in Ireland, tracing his journey up the Boyne River, his landing in Drogheda, his meeting with a pagan King and finally celebrating Easter Sunday Mass on the Hill of Tara. This was right up Mac's street with his attraction to the pageantry and rituals of the Catholic Church. He'd loved playing Cardinal de Medici in *The Cardinal* and now to play Ireland's patron saint and sail up the Boyne in a replica of an ancient sailing vessel (actually motor powered) with thousands of admiring pilgrims following on, appealed to every theatrical bone in his body. Jack Dowling's experience in the army manoeuvering large companies of soldiers made him an ideal director, shouting commands through a loudspeaker as he rode around on horseback.

The pageant was a very spectacular production for Ireland with its limited resources, and it was a huge success (I was vaguely in it as a pagan princess) with thousands of people eventually gathering on the Hill of Tara. Some forgot that Mac wasn't really St. Patrick, and when he made the sign of the cross, (rather too broadly I thought) the crowd crossed themselves too and mothers held their children up to be blessed, but as Mac recalled, he kissed them, but didn't bless them. 'I drew the line there,' he said, 'I didn't want to be thought of as a heretic.' He looked magnificent – dressed in the robe of a bishop with a huge gold cross woven into the front of it, and on his head the tall white mitre, not historically correct, but he insisted on wearing it, because that is how St. Patrick is dressed in all the pictures of him in Ireland.

Mac was so delighted with the success of the pageant he resolved to do it again the next year, though there was no talk of the present producers repeating it. If necessary, Mac would produce it himself.

About this time, Mac began to work on *King Lear*, the only great Shakespearean character he wanted to do and hadn't yet. He was now 61 and over the years he'd studied *Lear* casually but not with any great focus. He hadn't wanted to play it he said until all remnants of youth had finally vanished. Now he was the right age and he knew if he waited much longer he might not have the physical stamina to do it. So once again the company and especially my little mother endured frustration and agony as Mac struggled to give birth to King Lear. Eventually after a protracted period of rehearsal, Lear went on and he played it up and down and across Ireland until he was comfortable enough not to have to think – until his face contorted – what his next line was. In Athlone, Harold, who was playing Edgar, wrote in his essay:

> He did Lear eventually ... knew most of the lines ... was the old man, tetchy, appalled, feverish. He wanted the storm louder. All of us banged the thunder sheets. No, they can still hear me. Hit it, hit it! He got above the noise ... At the centre of his performance was a terrible loss, desolation, silence. He didn't talk about doing it, he just got there. He did it and got there.

When Mac grew into the part, he was a monumental Lear; imperious, stoic, controlling, and infinitely pitiful when he is beset by Goneril and Regan. It was almost too much to bear watching his breakdown and descent into madness. 'Like a great fallen oak,' as Barry Foster described him. Christopher was the best Fool imaginable. The scenes between the two of them would make the hardest heart split in two.

Lear did exhaust my father. Though he was still strong and broad-shouldered, the emotional strain depleted him. It was an effort, too, for him to carry me as the dead Cordelia and he did it with a kind of savage determination as if his life depended on it. He was like an animal pushed beyond endurance.

In the early stages of *Lear*, my mother who came to know the lines of every new play Mac was in, hid herself under a rostrum in the storm scene, because Mac was especially uncertain of the words there. She knew him so well and his weakest spots, so from her hiding place, when the time came, she'd whisper the line to him. She had no script or flash-light, she just crouched there – ready. This is another small example of their partnership. He could not have done it all without her, and she could not have lived her life without him.

I was fond of Cordelia, but I found the role difficult. There is such a long gap between the first scene when she tells her father, 'I love your majesty according to my bond, no more, nor less', and then she's banished and doesn't reappear until half the play is over. It was hard to start cold again. Then too, I knew it was a physical strain for Mac to carry me, and being horizontal always triggered my cough, and Mac was too distraught, or uncertain, to cover it up as he had in Othello. It was quite an ordeal for both of us!

We toured, of course, through the rest of 1953 and most of 1954. In October, Mac felt he was ready to play his *Lear* in Dublin and a two week engagement at the Gaiety Theatre was arranged for a full week of *Lear* and his new production of *The Taming of the Shrew* for the second week. However, Louis

Elliman, the General Manager of the Gaiety predicted that two plays only would not bring in the crowds and insisted Mac do at least three more, so as well as *Lear* and *The Shrew*, we did *Othello*, *The Merchant*, and *Hamlet*, and we packed the Gaiety from floor to ceiling for the entire run. We opened with three nights of *King Lear*, the only time Mac ever played it in Dublin. The reviews were all good with special praise for Christopher's Fool. Next came two performances of *Hamlet*, remarkable because they would be the last time my father ever played the part. He'd played *Hamlet* from the early days of his career, almost 30 years, but now at 62 he didn't want to be thought of as 'mutton dressed as lamb,' as he said in his curtain speech. It was time to let it go.

As Mac had had in mind only two productions originally at the Gaiety, he'd put a lot of time and energy into the new production of *The Shrew*. He set it in Ireland with sets of thatched cottages and hillsides designed by Kay Casson, Lord Longford's set designer since they began. Hilton directed it with an eye on bawdiness and plenty of fun. In the cast was Milo O'Shea, the well-known and much loved actor who played Grumio with a gorgeous 'gutty' Dublin accent.

I remember those two weeks with nostalgia and gratification. We were playing in the Gaiety, the most beautiful and comfortable of Dublin's theatres. The houses were packed. The notices were unanimous and glowing in their praise. I was playing all my 'very own' parts. The company was happy and full of fun. Jack and I were on as firm a footing as we ever were, and were becoming closer (in spite of the subtle disapproval I felt from my parents) and we were in Dublin, the city I adored.

Jack, like many actors, had an ego and though he admired Mac enormously, he wasn't altogether pleased that I had him on such a high pedestal. He wanted my praise and said until I broke the umbilical cord that tied me to my parents I'd not be my own woman! Partly to prove him wrong, after the Gaiety we went to London where we rented a dingy little flat in Warrington Crescent. The house, like rows and rows of others just like it, had once been an elegant Victorian dwelling for the fairly affluent but had since fallen on hard times and was now portioned off into five or six miserable little 'studios'. Ours had a bath in the kitchen, covered when not in use with a large piece of plywood, as if it could be disguised!

I was still 'backward in going forward' as Mac said of me, and I felt enormously guilty about 'living in sin' with Jack. Yes, by this time we were living in 'connubial bliss'. At 27, I'd finally taken the plunge! In spite of not being 'in a state of grace', I went faithfully to Mass every Sunday, but didn't receive communion. I wondered if I was past redemption and prayed for my soul when Jack wasn't there.

Back in Ireland, Mac once again was St Patrick in the pageant. This time he produced it and this time it was held in Croke Park, the huge football stadium on Dublin's northside. He invited Hilton to direct it and Micheál to write the script, which he did, including long sentences in Irish that 'flummoxed' my father and which he cut to a minimum. It was a giant undertaking and as always my mother was realistically the producer and was ultimately responsible for the coordination of the massive crowds, the costumes, the music, and the actors.

The pageant at Croke Park drew enormous crowds and once again Mac revelled in it, the character that is, but he didn't enjoy it as he had the year before because, as Mana wrote for him in the *Times* articles:

> ... the magic was missing. The Boyne River, Slane and Tara (the actual locals of Patrick's journey), seem to hold a remnant of those far off days when St. Patrick came sailing up the river and changed the face of Ireland.'

Within days after the pageant was over, Mac was on tour again, but the enthusiasm and gaiety that usually exuded from him seemed to be waning. 'Perhaps he's just getting tired,' my mother wrote to me, 'He's not paying attention to rehearsals – he seems to want to get them over as soon as possible.' I think he knew well the writing was on the wall, that his way of life and what he loved doing most, was coming to an end. Not touring would be a death sentence for Mac, stripping him of all that was safe and familiar. Still, he kept going for the present with the essential help of monies he'd earned with the success of the Gaiety season and the pageant, but it was only 'band-aiding' the situation. He knew it and it depressed him deeply.

Advertising, rental of halls and theatres, transportation, actors' salaries, hotels and digs, Equity's demands, expenses of every kind were all making it impossible to continue, and though business was still generally good, the revenue wasn't enough to keep the company afloat.

It's extraordinary that no subsidy was ever offered to my father by the government. Mac never spoke of it, but he must have been chagrined that the Abbey who had been receiving a subsidy, small though it was, in the beginning, was now ever being increased as the years went by. Even harder to swallow was that the Gate was now being subsidized, but Micheál and Hilton had lobbied for it relentlessly and they had had half the ministers in the Dáil manoeuvering for them! Mac, who was probably the least conniving person I ever knew, didn't go after it and he was too grand to apply for it! Look too much like begging, so he 'cut off his nose to spite his face'. They struggled on. The company was reduced to about 8 or 9 actors and was reminiscent of conditions during the war.

It didn't help matters that when the company had been out just a few weeks another fire hit in the Autumn of 1955, this time to Skibbereen Co. Cork, burning the hall and most of the props, costumes, and sets. It might have been time then to call it quits, but no such thought entered Mac's head and the company played *Dial M For Murder*, in Bantry Co. Cork only a couple of days after the fire.

About this time my parents gave up the flat in Fitzwilliam Square and bought a beautiful little Georgian house on Sandymount Strand in Dublin. It was the first piece of property they had ever owned and with what they bought it I have no idea, but Mac, being as respected and well-known as he was, probably had no difficulty borrowing from various Irish Banks.

In London, after several months of doing odd jobs and going to the theatre and opera as much as we could afford to, Jack was suddenly faced with the possibility of losing his U.S. citizenship, having been in Europe over 7 years and almost overnight he needed to return to America. The events of the next few days happened so swiftly that they seemed entirely unreal.

The day of Jack's departure to America, we were married unceremoniously, in Marylebone Registrar's Office on July 25th 1955, the very same one that my parents were married in 30 years before! I phoned Sally, who was living in London at the time, to come and be a witness, but I was unable to reach her – not one member of my family was present! This couldn't really be actually happening. Jack phoned Arthur Klein, an old friend from his university days and he came, and we waylaid a stranger who was walking by to be the other witness!

That evening, I waved Jack goodbye as he boarded a train for Southampton en route to New York. And there I was, alone in London, wondering what on earth I had done! It didn't seem real. It's all a weird dream, I thought. I'd go home to Ireland and wake up on tour.

Eventually, I found Sally and the two of us went off to Soho and ate curry! Wonderful free spirited Sally, but even she questioned what I had done. 'Are you sure you've done the right thing?' she said. I wasn't, but I'd done it, and I had to face reality. I loved Jack, but whether we were suited to spend our lives together was a *big* question mark.

I wired my parents, 'Got married today, love, Mary-Rose' and in the next day or two I went back home to Ireland, to the reality I knew, home to Ireland.

My mother was not pleased. 'Your grammar is so bad,' she said. 'You can't say 'got' married. 'Was' married or we 'were' married, but *not* 'got' married!' She could have said bluntly 'Marrying Jack was not a good idea.' She didn't, but I knew that was what she felt.

Mana liked good manners and Jack's were rough. He had a 'casual' way of behaving and dressing that I thought was typically American, but which could have seemed inappropriate. Mostly she disapproved because Jack was experienced and I was an innocent, 'unsifted in such perilous condition'. She knew we would not have a 'comfortable' life and I think she wondered if he would be faithful to me.

Mac was silent except for mumbling. It was a good thing I'd done it in a Registrar's office and not in the church, but I knew by the set look on his mouth that he wasn't pleased. Even Chris, who was always my friend, said caustically, 'You've burnt your bridges, Mary-Rose.'

As the weeks went by, it entered my head that I might be pregnant and I went to a doctor. 'Oh yes,' he said, 'There's definitely a baby on the way.' 'But I can't be,' I said. 'We were together such a short time.' 'It only takes one time,' said the doctor kindly, trying not to show he must be talking to a lunatic.

Was it a dream? I couldn't actually be married, or that I'd have to leave Ireland and live in America, perhaps forever! Glory, what *had* I done? But like everything in my life, I hadn't thought it through. I was so like my father. How many times had he gone headlong into something with no thought of the consequences? Spur of the moment decisions, like leaving London for Australia the first time, not giving a thought to what his absence would do to his budding career. But Mac had a guardian angel who watched out for him, and his decisions, however scatty they seemed, usually turned out to be right for him. I'm not sure it was so for me! I've wondered whether, if I'd considered the ramifications, I would have married Jack so quickly. I'd be going to a country I felt no attraction for, leaving my own which I loved so much and the touring life that was as much a part of me now, as it was for my parents. And yet somewhere in my subconscious was a need for change, I had toured now for 17 years, would I go on touring until I was 'old and grey and full of sleep?' Did Mac and Mana expect me to run the company one day? That is, if there was still a company to run! Poor Daddy. He was having to face changes in his way of life, and now he must have felt abandoned by both his children, for later that year Chris married Jill Gotts, an aspiring young actress who joined the company not long before I left it. He found a good position directing for Granada television and moved permanently to England.

25 – I Leave the Company

For a short time, I rejoined the company while waiting for Jack to find some work and a roof over our heads, but the aura had changed for me. I was no longer really a member of the company. My parts had all been given away and I played some smaller ones just to earn my keep.

All this is as it should be, but I couldn't help feeling resentment that others were playing my parts, wearing my costumes, and speaking the lines I loved. I had to detach myself. I was clinging onto something that was not mine anymore and it was painful. I was saying goodbye to the only life I'd ever known. But eventually, the inevitability of it took over and I finally had to let go. So it was leaving my father's company. Tears of resentment for Jack that I had to, but in the end a feeling of exhilaration that I was beginning a new phase – a new adventure.

If this was my biography, I'd describe the perils of being pregnant and being the only female on a cargo ship. Contending with rolling, lurching waves, a drunken absentee captain, and no one on board with any knowledge of medicine – well, it seems that I have told you. But that's enough of me, at least for a time.

Mac and Mana were getting along very well without me which shows that we are all expendable. My parts were divided between Tressa Curley, a talented and unusual young actress from Dublin and my not-yet-sister-in-law, Jill. As usual a handful of new people joined, and a few left. These I never knew but they stayed with the company until the very last tour. One was Nancy Manningham, an English actress who Mac came to rely on more and more. She played most of the leading ladies and directed too when Mac didn't.

Late in 1955, Mac ventured into Northern Ireland, a rare event since he had the fixed idea that the Presbyterian citizens of the 'Black North' hated the theatre and especially Shakespeare, so he'd steered clear of it. Why he changed his mind to go, I can only guess. The north was more solvent than the south at the time – being backed by the British and having more industry – and things were getting tougher all the time in the south.

The company visited eight good-sized towns and in spite of Mac's gloomy predictions, was a huge success. 'We seem to be a nine-day wonder' wrote my mother, to Gabriel Fallon (friend, critic, and a director of the Abbey Theatre) ' ... out of this', she continued, 'came an offer from the British Council for the Encouragement of Music and Art (CEMA) offering us a guarantee against loss for future tours, ... and the hope that the McMaster Company would make annual visits to Northern Ireland! Isn't it a joke?'

It was a joke 'designed to break the heart', wrote Carl Falb in his thesis. How ironic. The Republic of Ireland, so well-known for its writers, actors, and love of the arts; and Ulster, generally less responsive to them, should be the ones to give Mac support!

The amount offered was not large and it meant that if Mac made money CEMA would give him nothing, but the gesture had been made and Mac was grateful.

Back in the south, my parents struggled once again with Equity's demands. Even the minimum salary for actors was becoming impossible to meet. And, once again, the company went on the commonwealth system of sharing the profits after expenses were paid. And so the company tottered precariously along. Mana wrote to me in New York (that) ' ... Mac was in a permanent state of gloom. The only time he comes to life is when he's acting one of the great parts and then the old enthusiasm and sparkle returns to his eyes.'

I noted before I left that the company was less strong than usual and smaller. How long could the company continue to tour? Would it all come to an end in a whimper? Would it not have been prudent to stop with the Gaiety season, on the crescendo of success, when the company was one of the strongest we'd ever had?

In February, 1957, Mac and several members of the company joined Micheál and Hilton at the Gaiety Theatre in a modern dress production of *Julius Caesar*. Hilton directed and played the name part. Micheál miscast himself as Anthony and Mac was Brutus. The critic of *The Irish Times* wrote of him '... (he gave) a deeply moving interpretation ... catching every stage of the initial struggle between love and duty.' After the two-week run which played to full houses, in spite of Mr Elliman's usual misgivings, Mac went back on tour.

Mana suggested that they disband the company and Mac should do a 'bits and pieces' tour: scenes, speeches and soliloquies of Shakespeare, a solo program he'd occasionally done for colleges and convents, but until it was absolutely necessary, they would keep on touring and they went once again to Ulster, but Mac's heart wasn't in it. He found it difficult, like me, to accept change, especially the end of things, and yet what is the theatre but constant change – for most – but for Mac there had been constancy in touring, doing mostly the same plays he'd always done, revisiting the same towns. It had seemed reasonably secure and the thought of it ending was frightening to him.

But the theatre, too, is full of extraordinary surprises, and just as touring in the north, even as a guarantee against loss, was nearing its end Mac was suddenly catapulted into a new and exciting world he'd never dreamt of. A place of tall buildings that almost reached the sky, of television interviews and high-powered publicity, of intensive rehearsals, and new faces and new cities. He was going to America!

26 – America and *Long Day's Journey*

'Don't go into the theatre,' said my father, 'unless it's too painful and unthinkable not to.' True, it's hard to think of an occupation that offers less security and one needs an extra dose of self-confidence or be insensitive to battle the disappointments and rejection, but it can also offer unexpected excitement too, which makes it all worthwhile.

So it was for Mac as he toured rather drearily from one stoic little town to another in the 'black north'; how could he have known that in a matter of days, he'd be whisked off to New York, to a country he'd never set foot in and hadn't ever thought to visit.

It happened that one day, out of the blue, came a telegram from the New York producers of Eugene O'Neill's play, *Long Day's Journey into Night*, offering Mac the part of James Tyrone on the U.S National tour. Both my parents imagined at first it must be some mistake or someone's warped idea of a practical joke, for how would producers in New York even know of my father or how to contact him?

Long Day's Journey, Eugene O'Neill's autobiographical and last play, had been a huge success on Broadway and starred Frederick March and Florence Eldridge as James and Mary Tyrone, the names O'Neill gave his parents in the play.

It had gone to the Paris Theatre Festival and later reopened in New York, almost two years of non-stop performances. March was exhausted and when it came to the U.S. National tour, he bowed out.

Replacing March presented difficulties; he'd created the part and was identified with it and some good character actors in New

York who may have been quite suitable probably would not present themselves for fear of being compared unfavourably with March. The producers, José Quintero and Theodore Mann were in a quandary as to what to do. It was all settled one evening at Sardi's, the famous theatrical restaurant, when the producers discussed the situation with Siobhán McKenna, who was playing in New York at the time. She recommended Mac and said she could think of no one more suitable to play a retired actor than him. Sight unseen and not having ever heard his name before, they decided to offer Mac the part – if they could find him, for no one seemed to know where he was.

Eventually Dermot Doolan tracked Mac down after contacting a lawyer in the North whose name was Andrew McMaster and no relation, who agreed to find him. After that, Mac was in a whirlwind of travel arrangements and trans-Atlantic phone calls as he and the producers discussed details and his salary, which Mac couldn't 'fathom' because they were talking in dollars not pounds, and in three days he was on a plane bound for New York.

Mana, as usual, thinking of only what was good for Mac decided to stay at home to keep things going. It was a decision she must have known wasn't right. She knew that Mac didn't function well without her and I wonder she didn't insist on going with him. Again, it would have been a good time to end the touring life and disband the company, but she also needed to keep Mac's flame alive. What had he to come home to if the company was gone?

In New York, meanwhile, I was struggling with homesickness and the extremes of the weather. The cold was more penetrating than any I'd felt in Ireland, and the humid heat was excruciating in the summer. Jack had found work in the theatre off-Broadway soon after I arrived and I was getting more rotund by the minute. Things were going fairly well if only I could deal with the homesickness I felt. Sometimes when Jack was rehearsing I'd go down to the docks and cry as I watched the ships being slowly towed out of the harbour on their way back to Europe.

Poor Jack, he needed a supportive optimistic wife and I wasn't at the time. New York was overwhelming to me, overcrowded and very dirty, at least it was where we lived on the upper west side. Money was tight, we lived on the edge of not knowing how we would pay the rent or where the next job was coming from, but we were young and Jack was full of ambition and fun, and when things were looking rather grim he always made me laugh. 'A sense of humour is essential to a happy marriage,' my mother once said, and we were particularly broke when it came time for our first child to be born.

John David was born in the middle of the night in St Vincent's Hospital in Greenwich Village after we stopped hurriedly at some actor friends' home for money to pay for the taxi. The baby was perfect in every way, but when it was time to take him home, the hospital demanded $300.00 before they would release him! 'What are you going to do, keep the baby hostage?' asked Jack, but he had a way with him and of course the three of us left together.

God is good and provides and Jack landed a good job instructing a Shakespeare course at the American Academy of Dramatic Art and I occasionally substituted for him when he had an audition. I felt myself able to do so, after all I had acted in Shakespeare for over 17 years, except that as I'd never heard of iambic pentameter, I couldn't explain it!

Mana wired me that Mac was on his way to New York and to be sure to meet him, and with Boodie (John's nickname, pronounced as in wood) I did. Mac was relieved to see me and greeted me with a lovely hug. 'What are you doing darling?' he asked. I knew he'd have no idea that taking care of a baby was all consuming and if I'd answered that that's what I was doing, he'd probably have asked 'but what are you really doing?' So I answered that I sometimes substituted for Jack teaching Shakespeare to students (how can one *teach* Shakespeare?) 'Ah, yes, muttered my father, 'the blind leading the blind.'

I realized something, probably for the first time: that my father hardly knew me! I suppose it's understandable. He was such a theatrical buoyant personality and I'd been a hesitant shy little girl for so long. What would we have talked about? Even as I grew older, our relationship was more professional than personal, but now I had interests and opinions and a little family of my own and I wanted to be able to talk to him as an adult. It made me sad. I loved him and admired him as an actor more than any other, and I felt knew him almost as well as my mother, but he knew me hardly at all.

27 – Home Again and More Changes

I'd been in New York several months by now and though I disliked it, it had become less alien to me as I became more familiar with it. I loved the museums and especially the Metropolitan Opera, and I slipped off to it every chance I could. (Now, there is something my father and I could have talked about, for we both loved it.) I saw Maria Callas in *Norma*, *La Somnambula*, and *Lucia di Lammermoor*. (Her voice was not always beautiful, but what an actress!) I saw Giuseppe di Stefano, Carlo Bergonzi and Mario del Monaco, glorious voices all of them. I saw Renata Tebaldi, and Licia Albanese, who was not beautiful but her soprano had a delicacy and sweetness that I've never quite heard since. She was the perfect Puccini heroine. I took Mac to see the great Zinka Milanov in *La Forza del Destino* in the midst of his heavy rehearsal schedule. It was the most memorable performance and production I've ever heard of that opera, and now still whenever I hear the overture, I think of Mac and cry a little. This era seemed to me the golden age of opera and continued to the next generation with Pavarotti, Domingo, and José Carreras, a favourite of mine, who (if one can compare and one shouldn't) didn't have the fullness of tone of Pavarotti or perhaps the strength of Domingo, but a lovely sensitivity and warmth. I saw Leontyne Price, Mirella Freni, and Joan Sutherland, with her extraordinary coloratura, to name a few. I've not forgotten any of them, and this golden age lasted until the early 80s when for me it ended and nothing nowadays can reach quite the same heights. Is it that I'm in the 'old people's syndrome' of thinking that things were so much better in the 'old days', or has the standard really deteriorated? One thing is sure,

I'm very blessed to have seen and heard some of the greatest singers of any generation.

Spring in New York is the loveliest time and especially Central Park, the wonderful leafy oasis in the middle of the madness of the city. Everywhere, blossoms and buds of every kind; huge beds of daffodils and tulips all springing to life reminding us again that God and nature, not man, are in charge.

In the glory of this island of sanity, with Boodie in his pram, I walked with my father every morning as I tried to help him memorize the lines of *Long Day's Journey*. As usual it was agonizing and I didn't have Mana's sixth sense of knowing when he was going to 'dry'. I tried to be as patient as I could but both of us felt irritable and frustrated by the end of a session.

It was a trying time for Mac, for me too, and Jack wasn't altogether happy that I was spending so much time with my father. Mac knew of course that a great deal depended on his performance. He was nervous as most actors would be in the same circumstances, but many would overcome that with self-confidence and discipline. Discipline had been ingrained in him as a young man. He used it but was not aware of it, now he needed to be very aware of it if he was to memorize and know this long part in 3½ weeks. As to his self-confidence, that was always tenuous if he felt he was being scrutinized as he did in Stratford years before. He knew he'd eventually play the part of James Tyrone. His misgiving was in the process of getting there and there was so little time. The pressure was intense and he was without Mana. The play was long and O'Neill's widow refused to allow a word to be cut. Great play that it is it is also an endurance test, watching the decline of four dysfunctional and despairing people.

After three weeks rehearsal, hardly enough I would think, for such a difficult work, *Long Day's Journey* had its first performances in Cleveland for a week, then on to Detroit for two weeks, both tryout dates to get the production ready for the official opening in Chicago.

In Chicago, Mac sent for Mana; it was no good, he couldn't do without her. She came at once, perhaps knowing very well that this would happen.

Mac's reviews were positive so far, but he didn't read them. The smallest criticism would affect his performance and bring about a state of depression, but Mana was there now and all would be well. She would talk sometimes about the need for Mac to have a thicker skin and not be so sensitive, but she was always there to shield him against any kind of adversity. She knew, I suppose, that we can't really alter our nature.

The play opened at the Erlanger Theatre in Chicago to a dismally small audience, and Claudia Cassidy, the respected and influential critic of *The Tribune* newspaper, wrote:

> One of the great plays of a lifetime came to the Erlanger on Monday and there were empty seats in the house ... (and) if we let it die here we have only ourselves to blame that the town is turning into a theatrical desert ... a powerhouse of a play, it has fallen into good hands. In Chicago as in New York it is magnificently acted and so superbly staged it just seems to happen.

In spite of good reviews, *Long Day's Journey* was still playing to small houses and the closing notice was posted. It was then that Claudia Cassidy went on a crusade to save it and enlisted the help of other critics, a radio station, and the popular Irv Kupcinet talk show on television. The happy result was that the box office receipts doubled the second week and it was decided that the tour should continue.

Chicago in December and January 'is not fit for human habitation' as Mrs Patrick Campbell might have said, with temperatures well below zero and a pitiless wind that blows off Lake Michigan 'tearing at one's face like claws' wrote my mother. The extremes in the weather were difficult for my parents. Inside was unbearably hot. 'We live in a hot house,' continued Mana, 'with the windows hermetically sealed and outside the cold would take your nose off.' Mana recalled going out only three times while they were in Chicago, except of course when they went to the theatre and this they did by taxi.

After five – eventually – good weeks in Chicago, the tour went to Pittsburg, a city that didn't attract Mana in the least and it too was very cold, and then off they flew to St Louis, where it was suddenly spring.

The tour was gaining momentum and was doing excellent business. The next date was Philadelphia, close enough for Jack and me to go there by train from New York to see it.

The part of James Tyrone is of an actor of the old school, retired now and disillusioned having played – for the sake of financial security – the same part all his professional life. Mac had a certain theatrical grandeur about him that seemed so right, but I could tell he wasn't 'under the skin' of the part yet, little things like not really listening to the other actor because he was thinking of what comes next! I knew in a few more weeks he'd take off and by all accounts he did. The critics were glowing, one remarking that one wholly believed him to be a retired actor, whereas Frederick March seemed more like a retired banker!

As Frederick March had had a huge success on Broadway, it was a challenge for any actor to step into his shoes. Mac didn't try! My father and March were entirely different personalities. They could hardly be compared unless one simply preferred one interpretation to the other. In a word, March's Tyrone was reserved, understated, and Mac's more theatrical.

The tour went to Washington D.C. – one of the high points of the tour. All was white and beautiful, with the neo-classical buildings gleaming in the spring sunshine and the glory of the cherry blossoms everywhere. Of special interest to Mac was Ford's Theatre where Lincoln was shot to death by the brother of one of Mac's heroes, the famous actor Edwin Booth. Mac was beginning to enjoy himself, but always the pressure of the coming evening performance weighed on him. Mac found the play, though undeniably one of the great dramas of the American theatre, excruciatingly depressing and too long. Only the presence of Mana stopped him from going to bed and staying there. Fay Bainter, well known in films of the 40s, who was playing Mary Tyrone, the drug addicted wife, also found the pressure intense and landed in the hospital with fatigue and pneumonia. Probably with a bit of pressure from the cast, the schedule of eight performances a week was reduced to seven.

The company played the National Theatre in Washington. (A few years later, Jack and I did *Dylan* there – a play about the poet Dylan Thomas.) The critics applauded the play and Richard Coe, of *The Washington Post* wrote:

> How does this compare with the company headed by Frederick March? I mean it when I say Miss Bainter and her Irish co-star satisfied me far more than I was [satisfied] that memorable Gotham evening of over a year ago.
>
> I did feel I wanted more for these two rich roles. Last night I felt I was getting what the printed version had led me to expect. This is McMaster's American debut and what an actor! He begins on not so high a note as March did ... and his voice is an

instrument to marvel about, a rich ranging of scale one seldom finds.

Another critic remarked that 'one was aware that he (Mac) was acting!' Generally speaking, this would be a criticism in another play with another character, but actors of the period were often just as dramatic off stage as well as on, (Micheál and Mac too, are witness to this) and it seems to me that James Tyrone would have been. Mac's interpretation was born out of the period he grew up in. It was not a conscious decision, it was natural for him to play it as he did.

In writing about Mac's characterization, Carl Falb finishes by saying, 'It is a tribute to McMaster that his Tyrone had no echo of Frederick March nor was it overwhelmed by comparison.'

The five-month tour eventually took the company on to Baltimore, Columbus, Denver and finally to Los Angeles and San Francisco.

'San Francisco is the loveliest city of all', wrote my mother, and they had a wonderful time there. Mac went swimming every day at one of the beaches only a short drive from the city, and on binges of 'squandermania' in Chinatown. The company was invited to all kinds of soirées, some in enormous and opulent houses given by the 'social set' of San Francisco. 'Only at night', Mana wrote, in the *Times* articles for Mac, 'and I came nearer to being James Tyrone again, the probing terror of the play began to get me in its grip as it always did. It repelled me and fascinated me at the same time.' (Quite melodramatic for Mana!)

Jack had long connections with San Francisco. His parents had lived there for more than forty years and still did. Jack's mother Alice, a fifth generation Californian whom I loved, had an air of vagueness that made her seem in wonder about everything around her. One evening she went to see *Long Day's Journey* and afterwards visited Mac in his dressing room which was filled with people. Overcome with shyness and without being seen, she hid behind the door. Eventually all the others left but she was too embarrassed to come out. Mac closed the door and there she was! Nervously, she introduced herself, and he coaxed her out of hiding by offering her a stiff drink. After that, Alice and Mac settled into a happy chat.

Los Angeles, the last stop of the tour was rather an anti-climax after the beauty of San Francisco. 'A city without a centre,' wrote Mana, 'it just stretches on in all directions like the tendrils of an octopus', but that it was exciting and full of energy. They looked up some old theatre friends who had come to Hollywood for work and were now part of the so-called 'British Colony'. They toured Warner Brother's studios and met Rosalind Russell and Gregory Peck. The play did good business there, and then it was all over and Mac and Mana flew straight to New York and then on to Dublin. They were home again and America was a distant memory.

28 – The Writing on the Wall

The company had tottered along, managed in Mac's absence by Nancy Manningham, whom Mac had come to rely on more and more, and Ronald Govey, actor and sometimes business manager; and only a few days after coming home Mac rejoined them in Limerick where a banner had been stretched across O'Connell Street announcing 'Mac's back!' He had returned to the routine without a ripple – doing what he loved best.

However, it was obvious that things had not improved economically, and once again Mac used his earnings, this time from *Long Day's Journey*, to keep the company going. They continued to tour until the end of 1958 and then sadly as if heralding his own demise, he and Mana decided the spring tour would be the last. The spring tour was only five weeks long and business wasn't good. At the end of it was another two week season at the Gaiety but it, too, was hardly the triumph the previous seasons had been. Mac gave his last performance in Ireland of Othello, the part he was most celebrated for. He had played it more than 2,000 times over a span of thirty-four years. He still had the vitality and strength to do it, though occasionally he cut the scene when he falls down in a fit! *The Irish Times* critic wrote:

> Anew McMaster himself emerges as a force and is something of a legendary figure ... His voice remains an instrument of astonishing range, his presence can still command, subdue and inspire an audience in the grand manner. Best of all, McMaster has a growing integrity in what he does, a faith in Shakespeare that brings its own reward in a strength and warmth with a great deal of subtlety. Much of the festival may be clumsy,

underdone, verging on the monstrous: the rest is vibrant, exciting and very much worthwhile.

Mac was somehow letting go. He'd always wanted the actors he was playing with to be as good as they could be. As Hilton once remarked, 'One didn't support Mac, one did a duet with him.' Barry Foster, in the BBC Tribute said:

> You learned by having to exist on the same stage as Mac. You had to appear as if you actually existed! He wanted you to exist. He wanted the ball to come over the net low and fast and right in the corner. He was very anxious that his Iago should be strong and attractive and in every way matching his brilliance. There was never any question of anyone taking a play from him.

But that had changed. Now it seemed his concentration and interest was only on his own performance, and he was giving little time to direction or even to the quality of acting of the other actors; he was detaching himself in a fatalistic way. If he couldn't do what he'd always done, then he was perhaps unconsciously hurrying the process of ending it. Mana was sometimes impatient with him, 'You're alive aren't you', she'd say, 'get up and go for a walk. I will not put up with this maudlin nonsense.' But Mac was facing old age too and he hated it. And if the time came that he could no longer act then there would be no point in living. If only he'd had other resources like Micheál to fall back on. What was in the future for him? Touring the colleges and schools with his 'bits and pieces' programme? It was a dismal outlook. Had he forgotten so quickly how unexpectedly he'd been invited to America? Something interesting could happen again. Micheál once said that 'Mac was either riding on the crest of his own enjoyment or he was in complete despair and life wasn't worth living.'

I think of my little mother in times like these. She was rather fragile now and needed someone to keep her going but all her energies were directed in keeping Mac afloat. She wrote me quite often. I was an outlet for her I think, someone to whom she could express her feelings. At home, she had to maintain a positive attitude, a cheery smiling appearance for Mac and for the people who visited. Sometimes in her letters she sounded defeated. She was just as anxious about the future as Mac was. I wanted to be with her, she had always been the one to give care, first to

Micheál and a lifetime with Mac. Now it was her time to be looked after and she was confiding in me! So long she had kept her feelings and thoughts hidden, never really exposing herself, not to me and Chris anyway. Now she seemed to need me in some way and I was glad; the problem was I was far away.

Jack managed to keep us going, teaching, going on tour, doing Summer Stock and we were happy. Life still stretched out in front of us and we were eager and optimistic. I was pregnant again but lost the baby after getting German measles, and in 1959, 3½ years after Boodie, my beautiful blue-eyed little daughter was born. Her birth 'is in my memory locked', for who could ever forget Micheál – who was playing in New York at the time in *Much Ado About Nothing* with John Gielgud – dashing into the hospital looking like the Prisoner of Zenda with his long black cape, the wide brimmed velour hat and the layers of makeup. He carried bunches of grapes and flowers and laid them down on my bed. 'Darling,' he said. 'How clever you are, and how brave – was it agony? What are you going to name her?' I told him Jack liked the name Jennifer. 'No, definitely no,' Micheál said defiantly, 'It's so terribly Anglo-Saxon darling. She shall be called Sinéad.' We tried it, but no one in the U.S. could pronounce it at the time, and she became Jenny.

It was lovely to see Micheál in New York. He was so assured and being possessed of a strong personality he didn't allow himself to be swallowed up in the vastness and facelessness of New York like me. After the run of *Much Ado*, he flew to Hollywood to make the film *What Ever Happened to Baby Jane*, and we moved to New Jersey suddenly and dramatically after finding rat droppings in Jenny's crib!

I was worried about my parents. How alone they must feel. No company, no Christopher, no me, and Micheál far away. Then suddenly we were going back to Ireland which of course delighted me, but was marred by the circumstances that made us decide to go. A doctor in New York had advised me to have my left lung removed! After a lifetime of coughing my lung was just sitting there, doing nothing and becoming more and more infected. It seemed out of the question to have the operation in the U.S. where the health care system, even in those days, was outrageously expensive. Even transporting the family back to Ireland and having the operation there was less costly than it would have been in America.

Mac and Mana invited us to stay with them in Sandymount which we did until we found a flat in Sandycove. I'd thought to give my mother the support she needed. Instead, as usual, she was the one to give support. I was pregnant again and I was about to have a major operation. Jack was having to work and look after Boodie, and Mana took Jenny, then about 14 months old, to stay with them. This must have been a gargantuan task for her and for Mac. They knew nothing about children and both were 'declined in the veil of years'.

My lung was taken out at Blanchardstown Hospital when I was four months pregnant. My mother came quite often to see me and I remember how strained and tired she looked. 'Jenny keeps going upstairs on all fours,' said Mana, 'and I'm going up after her a dozen times a day.' Poor little Mana, it was all physically too much – and she had Mac too – her only child!

A few months later my tiny brown-eyed daughter was born at the Rotunda Hospital in Dublin. My father had driven me there (at a snail's pace, which was the way he always drove in spite of my labour pains becoming closer by the second!) and he stayed until she arrived. Then he came in to see me, a stole around his neck and a prayer book in his hand. Ceremoniously he made the sign of the cross, 'In nomine Patris et Filii et Spiritus Sancti', he muttered piously,' I christen you Bernadette.' But, it wasn't to be because Jack and I wanted her to be Brigid Moira. She was baptized in the little Catholic church in Sallynoggin and Jack and I were married again there, five years and three children after the first time!

Brigid was not the sum of our family. Some months later number four was on its way! When he heard, Mac remarked 'Will she never stop? She goes on – and on – and on – and on, like the river Euphrates.' My beautiful David Christopher was born in San Francisco, where we went after Jack had applied for and received a grant to join a repertory company there.

Now we had two Davids in the family! Jack said it showed a pitiful lack of imagination, but I wanted one of the boys to be known as David, and Boodie was beginning to be called John.

God blessed us with these treasures, our four precious children and I've loved them with all my heart, but I never felt myself worthy or equipped to be their mother and sadly Jack didn't turn out to be the best of fathers.

Meanwhile, Mac was rallying. He had heard that the Abbey had obtained the rights to *Long Day's Journey* and were about to produce it. His success with the play in the U.S. had been noted in the Dublin newspapers and it would seem a natural rite of passage for Mac to be invited to play James Tyrone, but he wasn't. The uncharming Ernest Blythe, who was director of the Abbey at the time, said that it wasn't the policy of the Abbey to engage guest artists (true then, but later changed) and he cast Philip O'Flynn, a veteran of the company to play the part. Blythe, of course, could have made an exception, he was the policy maker. Whatever his reason, Dublin never saw Mac as James Tyrone. However, it wasn't the end of it for Mac; and, thank goodness, he'd had such trouble learning the lines and eventually becoming comfortable in the part, he wasn't ready to let it go. He made a radio recording of it and was later invited to play the part in England, by Gerald Batty, a former member of the company, who was now acting with a repertory company in Norwich. Mac was invited to direct as well. Off he went, his spirits lifted immediately. Yes, it was Norwich, a smoky provincial town, and it may have seemed dreary after the excitement of the U.S. tour, but it didn't matter, he was working.

Mac hadn't acted in England for 20 years and to his great surprise he was greeted by the cast as a celebrity. The play did well and he returned to Dublin glowing with satisfaction. It really wasn't difficult to make Mac happy.

In Dublin again he played in Shaw's *The Simpleton of the Unexpected Isles* for the second Dublin Theatre Festival. The critic of *The Irish Times*, remarked 'on the beautiful voices of the priest and priestess,' (she was Nancy Manningham) 'and their splendid presence that (almost) holds the play together!'

After 35 years of running his own company, Mac was now a freelance actor. He did a few days' work as a judge in a film made at Ardmore Studios. He played Long John Silver in 'a huge spectacular' production of *Treasure Island* staged in a boxing stadium and involving almost every actor in Ireland. It was not a success and ended after a weekend, and Mac was never paid.

About this time, my little mother became quite ill. This was unusual, for though she suffered from migraine headaches all her life, her general health was good. Once, she had shingles and she'd been in terrible pain. My father had rallied and did all he could think of for her, taking her to a specialist in Dublin, then to another in London. He had nuns and priests praying for her and when nothing seemed to do any good, in desperation he took her – a little skeptically – to Lourdes. There, with God's good grace she found relief – for about a year – then some pain, but not as bad – returned. Mac was very grateful to St Bernadette, which was the reason he wanted Brigid to be named after her.

Now, however, Mana was quite seriously ill again and she went to hospital. I've never found out what was actually wrong with her. I asked Christopher on one of his visits to us in California but he was typically vague. This was one of the few times my father ever wrote to me. His tone was anxious, he was frightened, and he needed support. I regret so much not going to Dublin to see my parents then and I should have, but it seemed out of the question at the time. I was seven thousand miles away on the west coast of America. I had four young children, the youngest only four months old. Jack's tenure with the Actor's Workshop had ended and we had started our own theatre. Jack and I did everything ourselves – it was a sink or swim endeavour. Yes, it would have been very difficult to leave but not impossible.

Micheál wrote to me that Mac almost lived at the hospital and that he could hardly be wrenched away. A poignant picture of Mac and my mother was drawn by the eminent playwright and actor, Emlyn Williams (who was playing in Dublin at the time with his one man show on Charles Dickens). He had not met either Mac or Mana before but he knew Micheál who introduced them.

> '... I'd heard a lot about Mac from his brother-in-law, Micheál, and I knew that Anew McMaster played Shakespeare superbly in the old grand manner, and half-expected a stately, handsome old boy with old grand manners, and an old grand voice. I found instead an eager, merry, ageless, agile Irish fellow – bright eyes and ringing laugh ... Marjorie, too, was a surprise; I'd envisaged Michael's sister as being on the massive side, and as ebullient as he is. Instead I was greeted by a shy, gentle wisp of an Irish girl as ageless as her husband. She looked like a third Gish sister; and as like her brother as milk is like quicksilver ... The next time I saw Mac was again in Dublin ... This time, over the merriment of lunches with Michael and Mac and Hilton, a shadow was cast which I'm now glad to have been with because it showed me another side of Mac. Marjorie was ill in hospital, and pretty ill, it seemed to me. One afternoon I took her flowers and as I walked there with Mac in

the spring sun he spoke a couple of lines from Othello, not for effect, but as if they were something belonging to him that he was remembering. Then he recalled something funny that had happened on a tour and, when we arrived, he was bubbling again. But, at his wife's bedside, he changed again. Marjorie did look ill, like a little girl who might easily be going to die. He perched next to her pillow, and the complex and gleaming mantle of the star actor had fallen from him like a coat; he sat there holding her hand, subdued, gentle, worried, caring. He was suddenly very simple. He was a dear man.'

Eventually Mana recovered, thank God, and Mac trotted off on tour again with his 'bits and pieces' programme, accompanied only by Olga, his beloved Samoyed, the daughter of Anna his previous dog. For a gregarious man who loved the company of his fellow actors, touring solo must have been deadly for him, but he put up with it, so long as Mana was there offering comfort and love when he returned. He did adjudicate for various amateur groups which he didn't like doing, but the fees were good. It galled him that he had to make money this way after so many years of bringing good theatre to the country and he showed the bitterness he felt in a speech at one of the amateur festivals. He pointed out that with all the government monies given to the Abbey, it had done almost nothing for audiences in the country, while after a lifetime he'd been forced to stop touring. Of course, he had a point, but in Mac's simple way of thinking, all was either black or white, no grays. The other contributing factors, such as expenses of every kind going forever up, difficulties with Equity, the competition of television, etc., Mac was not considering. The government and the Abbey was the enemy and that was that.

Mac kept going anyway he could, which was a blessing. Idleness deeply depressed him. [What was the point of getting up in the morning, bathing, shaving, getting dressed – for what?] These times were especially hard on Mana and she invited a steady flow of enthusiastic young actors and students to the house to keep him occupied. One of them was Matthew Diskin, a young man who lived down the street. Matt idolized Mac and Mana too. He and his family have remained friends to this day and we still keep in touch.

In 1961, Mac's only appearance in Dublin was in Ibsen's '*When We Dead Awaken*', hardly a play to lift Mac's spirits. It was apparently rather a strange production and that's all I know about it! 1962, however, Mac was really busy. He was judging the

Drama Festival in Limerick; he had a T.V. appearance; a midnight performance at the Gaiety for the benefit of the Equity Retirement Fund which included Micheál and Peter Ustinov, the well-known British actor; a second T.V. appearance reading the sonnets of Shakespeare, and going on a 'bits and pieces' tour whenever there was a hiatus. Then out of the blue came an invitation to play Othello from a former member of the company who was now artistic director of a repertory company in Farnham, a town about 40 miles from London. Delighted, Mac accepted, he would be playing his favourite part once more in England, perhaps for the last time.

It turned out to be a special time for Mac. The houses were packed for the whole week. The critics were enthusiastic, remarking, as usual, on Mac's remarkable voice. 'What a lesson to young actors,' wrote one; 'every sigh, every whisper audible ... It rises to sonorous grandeur at times of dramatic crises and falls to a caressing murmur as he loses Desdemona.' He was reunited with former members of his company and old friends he'd not seen for over 40 years, who came from all over England to see him. After the show, he and his retinue would congregate in the local pub; Mac was in his element. The week was a celebration somehow of Mac's 50 years in the theatre, and he was playing the part he was most celebrated for.

Mac returned to Sandymount in high spirits, and when the producers of two musicals, *The Maid of the Mountains* and *The Desert Song*, which were about to be staged at the Gaiety, suggested half-jokingly, that Mac should play the young hero in both of them, he happily accepted. Why not? The musicals were dated, to say the least, but Mac was delighted – one last chance to recapture his youth. I can just hear him saying 'On with the false piece (toupée), the number 9 (grease paint) makes one look gloriously juvenile again dear, the surprise pink follow spot, and away we go!' He was now 69 years old. Only in Dublin could he have gotten away with it!

In the autumn of 1962, Micheál and Hilton were producing *Othello* for the Dublin Theatre Festival and invited Mac – of course – to play Othello, with Micheál as Iago, Hilton as Brabantio and to direct. Afterwards, they planned to take the production to England and possibly the continent. Mac accepted, and agreed at Mana's insistence, to have a doctor look him over before embarking on what could be a strenuous schedule. Mac was 70 by now, still tall, unbent, broad shouldered, and as vigorous as ever, and when he was home, he kept up with his daily swim at the Forty Foot. He appeared to be the epitome of good health, but he was not. The doctor told him he had a blood clot in his upper right arm and to stay in bed and do as little as possible for the time being. Othello was definitely out.

At first, Mac played the part of the invalid with gusto, receiving friends and neighbours propped up on a dozen pillows and taking little breaths between words, to show how weak he was. Micheál came at once when he heard the news and wrote with his usual flourish how Mac greeted him:

> Oh, there you are Micky, I'm poorly as you might say, very poorly. The doctor looked askance at me ex-rays and told me to go to bed and stay there. I feel like Sarah dear, in *La Dame aux Camélias*.'

However, it wasn't long before the reality of his situation struck him; it was serious, the diagnosis was thrombosis, a clot of blood which, if it reaches the heart, is fatal.

The idea of being an invalid was out of the question and if he couldn't go on acting, then it was time to go – and after four days, he quietly died. Mac had always walked away from unpleasant situations and he was doing it now. Perhaps with treatment and rest he would have recovered, but like a child he wanted immediate results and he wasn't willing to wait. Perhaps if he'd thought of what his going would do to Mana he might have fought a little harder, but she had conditioned him to think only of himself and what was best for him. As it was, the suddenness of his death devastated her and though she went through the paces of living for the next seven years, it seemed she was only marking time until she could join him.

Mana was too shocked to go to the funeral, held at Star of the Sea church in Sandymount. Mac would have loved it. All of theatrical Dublin was there and hundreds who were his audiences from all over Ireland, as well as dignitaries from the government, bishops, and dozens of priests and nuns.

The family was represented by Christopher and his wife Jill, Micheál and Hilton, and cousin Sally. 'What a strange creature your brother is,' wrote Micheál, 'he seemed more interested in telling me about the invasion of Poland, than burying his father!'

I am sad, even now, that I didn't try harder to go. There is always a good reason but it doesn't alleviate the guilt I feel.

Two years later we were back once more in the country I love. Jack and I had had quite a success with the play *Dylan* and we'd taken it on a national tour in the U.S. Then after some negotiations back and forth, we were invited to do it at the Gaiety Theatre for the Dublin Theatre Festival. We brought our four children and stayed at first with Mana.

It was just what she needed. For a time she forgot her pain and became a loving and attentive grandmother. She talked to the children, read them stories, and played with them on the strand. Could it really be Mana? I was amazed and delighted. *Dylan* was again a success and we had some very good reviews from the press, but even if we'd not done it, the whole visit would have been worthwhile just to see Mana happy again.

I'm sorry that my children never really knew Mac, and now that they have lived almost all their lives in America they are far removed from 'those days' and the kind of theatre my father did. It is their heritage and I want them to know who he was ('A remarkable man of the Theatre' Noel Coward called him.)

He had been able to live his life as he wanted all the time. How many people can say that? There is always compromise along the way.

I truly believe that Mac was 'overseen' by a force that made the right decisions for him. Why should he need such a 'force', one might ask? Did he not make up his own mind like most people? No, because he was unable to deal with anything that needed to be seriously discussed or worked out. An undeveloped part of his brain? Or – and I think it more likely – a kind of mental laziness; he could have, but he didn't want to! He relied on what I've called his instinct, but it was more than instinct. He suddenly knew what was the best road to take; he couldn't have explained it, but it was always the right one for him.

Yes, there was a spirit, an angel keeping a close watch on my father, and when the touring life was finished, it let him know it was time to leave and he did. How blessed he was.

Related Literature

Brady, Frank, *Citizen Welles. A Biography of Orson Welles*, London 1990.

Falb, Carl, *A World Elsewhere. The Stage Career of Anew McMaster*, Ohio 1974. [Also: Theatre Arts Department, Ohio State University.]

Fitz-Simon, Christopher, *The Boys. A Double Biography*, Dublin 1994.

Mac Liammóir, Micheál, *All for Hecuba*, Boston 1961.

Ó hAodha, Micheál, *On the Importance of Being Micheál. A Portrait of Micheál Mac Liammóir*, Brandon, 1990.

Prentice, Penelope, *Harold Pinter: Life, Work, and Criticism*, York Press 1991.

www.ingramcontent.com/pod-product-compliance
Lightning Source LLC
Chambersburg PA
CBHW051613230426
43668CB00013B/2091